ANCIENT COMEDY

THE WAR OF
THE GENERATIONS

STUDIES IN LITERARY THEMES AND GENRES

Ronald Gottesman, Editor
University of Southern California

ANCIENT COMEDY

THE WAR OF
THE GENERATIONS

STUDIES IN LITERARY THEMES AND GENRES

Ronald Gottesman, Editor
University of Southern California

ANCIENT COMEDY

THE WAR OF
THE GENERATIONS

Dana F. Sutton

Twayne Publishers
New York

Maxwell Macmillan Canada
Toronto

Maxwell Macmillan International
New York   Oxford   Singapore   Sydney

H◆USTON PUBLIC LIBRARY

Ancient Comedy: The War of the Generations
Dana F. Sutton

Studies in Literary Themes and Genres No. 1

Copyright © 1993 by Twayne Publishers

Twayne Publishers   Maxwell Macmillan Canada, Inc.
Macmillan Publishing Company   1200 Eglinton Avenue East
866 Third Avenue   Suite 200
New York, New York 10022   Don Mills, Ontario M3C 3N1

Library of Congress Cataloging-in Publication Data

Sutton, Dana Ferrin.
  Ancient comedy : the war of the generations / Dana F. Sutton.
    p. cm.—(Studies in literary themes and genres ; no. 1).
  Includes bibliographical references (p.) and index.
  ISBN 0-8057-0957-6 (alk. paper)
  1. Classical drama (comedy)—History and criticism. 2. Aristophanes—
Criticism and interpretation. 3. Menander, of Athens—Criticism and interpreta-
tion. 4. Plautus, Titus Maccius—Criticism and interpretation. 5. Terence—
Criticism and interpretation. I. Title. II. Series.
PA3028.S88 1993   93-22912
882'.0109—dc20   CIP

10 9 8 7 6 5 4 3 2 1 (hc)

Printed in the United States of America

General Editor's Statement

Genre studies have been a central concern of Anglo-American and European literary theory for at least the past quarter century, and the academic interest has been reflected, for example, in new college courses in slave narratives, autobiography, biography, nature writing, and the literature of travel as well as in the rapid expansion of genre theory itself. Genre has also become an indispensable term for trade publishers and the vast readership they serve. Indeed, few general bookstores do not have sections devoted to science fiction, romance, and mystery fiction. Still, genre is among the slipperiest of literary terms, as any examination of genre theories and their histories will suggest.

In conceiving this series we have tried, on the one hand, to avoid the comically pedantic spirit that informs Polonius' recitation of kinds of drama and, on the other hand, the equally unhelpful insistence that every literary production is a unique expression that must not be forced into any system of classification. We have instead developed our list of genres, which range from ancient comedy to the Western, with the conviction that by common consent kinds of literature do exist—not as fixed categories but as fluid ones that change over time as the result of complex interplay of authors, audiences, and literary and cultural institutions. As individual titles in the series demonstrate, the idea of genre offers us provocative ways to study both the continuities and adaptability of literature as a familiar and inexhaustible source of human imagination.

Recognition of the fluid boundaries both within and among genres will provide, we believe, a useful array of perspectives from which to study literature's complex development. Genres, as traditional but open ways of understanding the world, contribute to our capacity to respond to narrative and expressive forms and offer means to discern moral significances embodied in these forms. Genres, in short, serve ethical as well as aesthetic purposes, and the volumes in this series attempt to demonstrate how this double benefit has been achieved as these genres have been transformed over the years. Each title in the series should be measured against this large ambition.

Ron Gottesman

Contents

Preface

I was extremely pleased to be invited to contribute a volume on ancient comedy by the editors of Twayne's *Studies in Literary Themes and Genres* series, since this offered me the opportunity to write a book that for some time I have thought should be attempted. Almost all accounts of ancient comedy stress the ways in which comedies of various periods differ from each other. On the other hand, for some time I have thought it would be interesting and profitable for us to focus our attention on the similarities that characterize all ancient comedy.

There are some visible reasons why the large majority of modern critics and literary historians are more impressed by the differences, which are admittedly numerous and striking. On the basis of very different subject matter and comic techniques, writers of later antiquity divided the history of Greek comedy into categories associated with distinct historical epochs: the Old Comedy of Aristophanes and his compeers, the Middle Comedy of the first half of the fourth century B.C., and the New Comedy of the latter half of that century and the first half of the next. By and large, modern successors of these early commentators have inherited this way of looking at things. The consideration that the various kinds of ancient comedy were produced under quite differing social conditions serves to reinforce the traditional view.

But if the differences are undeniable and impressive, we would be mistaken to permit them to obscure important similarities. If, viewed from some angles, the history of ancient comedy looks like a series of disjunct periods, if you look at it from other viewpoints it begins to seem much more continuous. I hasten to add that, due to the accidents of manuscript preservation and papyrological discoveries, we only have a comparative handful of ancient comedies, although it would be hard to imagine that the surviving plays by Aristophanes, Plautus, and Terence were not the best of the lot. Therefore the reader should be aware that all generalizations made in this book are founded on a small statistical sample, but a highly significant one.

In the present study, three important resemblances between earlier and later forms of ancient comedy are discussed to one degree or another, and one of these is selected as its underlying theme.

First, Greek Old and New Comedy and also Roman comedy are forms of so-called "festive comedy," to use the Shakespearean critic C. L. Barber's concept. Both the Old and New Comedies are rooted in the same holiday festivals consecrated to Dionysus, and Roman comedy was performed on various Roman holidays (*ludi*). This "festiveness" seems to be an important common denominator, to the point that the concept of festive comedy has become an important item in some recent comedy criticism. Following Barber's lead, some modern students of ancient comedy have suggested that festival comedies tend to have a characteristic spirit and viewpoint reflecting the festival holidays that served as their production contexts.

We can also speak about resemblances between different phases of ancient comedy in terms of the psychological mechanisms that come into play, of the ways comedy is intended to affect the spectator. Such concepts as comic catharsis, anxiety-reducing mechanisms such as self-referential metadrama and deliberate violation of dramatic illusion that create an emotionally safe environment, and deflating comic derision belong in this category. The different forms of ancient comedy can be compared to each other (and, of course also to comedy of other times and places) because the kinds of things that make spectators laugh, as comic writers know full well, are essentially similar. Prominent among these things are subversive comic attacks on social conformity and figures of authority who enforce, and often benefit from, such regimentation.

In the following pages I occasionally allude to some of these critical concepts, but not without a certain degree of discomfort. I am far from certain that as yet we have an adequate and commonly agreed-upon theoretical foundation for the criticism of comedy. Nor have we yet developed a wholly satisfactory mode of discourse in which such criticism can be conducted. In many of the more recent studies listed in the bibliography accompanying this study, one can see distinct advances toward construction of such a theoretical framework, which raise hopes that further progress in this direction can be expected. Surely such critical concepts as comic catharsis and metadrama will prove to be important components in any overall theory of comedy, and I strongly suspect that, the more such theories are proposed and discussed, the greater the effect they will have in drawing our attention to the similarities in ancient comedy.

There are also some common denominators involving thematic contents: the recurrent tension between country and city, for example, or the employment of cheeky and rebellious slaves. One such shared theme proves especially worth our consideration, because of the wealth of critical insight it yields. Although Aristophanes' primary focus is the wider world of the Athenian city-state, he occasionally takes a comic look at the subject destined to become the predominant concern of later Greek and Roman comedy, family life. Aristophanic comedy (sometimes) and New and Roman comedy (centrally) are concerned with generational conflicts within single families. Most often such conflicts involve fathers and sons, and indeed my first inclination was to write a book entitled *Fathers and Sons in Ancient Comedy*. The difficulty with that approach is that it would leave Menander rather out of the picture. The only one of his papyrological plays that deals with a father–son relationship is *Samia*, which is very imperfectly preserved, and I could not have discussed his *Dyscolus*, which is extant in near-perfect condition, if I had followed this original impulse. But if *Dyscolus* is not a father–son play, at least it is a play about a grumpy character who happens to be an oppressive father, and a play about the conflict of the old versus the young, or at least of the dysfunctional old against the wholesome young at heart. So I have widened my range in order to do more justice to Menander.

Chronology

486 B.C.   First comic competition at the Athenian Dionysia.

446 B.C.   Aristophanes born.

431 B.C.   Outbreak of the Peloponnesian War.

430 B.C.   Plague at Athens; Pericles dies.

426 B.C.   Aristophanes' first play, *The Banqueteers.*

425 B.C.   Aristophanes' *The Acharnians.*

424 B.C.   Aristophanes' *The Knights.*

423 B.C.   Aristophanes' *The Clouds* (original version—the version we possess is a somewhat later revision).

422 B.C.   Aristophanes' *The Wasps.*

421 B.C.   Aristophanes' *Peace.* The Peace of Nicias leads to a temporary suspension of the Peloponnesian War.

415–413 B.C.   A disastrous naval expedition to Sicily paves the way for the defeat of Athens in the Peloponnesian War

414 B.C.   Aristophanes' *The Birds.*

411 B.C.   Aristophanes' *Lysistrata* and *The Thesmophoriazusae.*

406 B.C.   Euripides dies. At his death he leaves behind the unperformed *Bacchae.*

405 B.C.   Aristophanes' *The Frogs.* Sophocles dies. For all intents and purposes, this spells the end of Attic tragedy as a vital literary form.

404 B.C.   Athens surrenders. From now to 371 B.C. the Greek world is to be dominated by the Spartan Hegemony.

ca. 400 B.C.   Beginning of the transition to Middle Comedy (signs of this change are visible in Aristophanes' last two plays).

392 or 391 B.C.   Aristophanes' *The Ecclesiazusae.*

388 B.C.   Aristophanes' *Plutus.*

385 B.C.   Aristophanes dies.

384 B.C.   Aristotle born.

358–336 B.C.   Reign of King Philip II of Macedon.

338 B.C.   Decisive defeat of Greece is forced by Philip. From now until absorption into the Roman Empire, Greece is to be dominated by Macedonian rulers.

ca. 342 B.C.   Menander born.

336–323 B.C.   Reign of Alexander III of Macedon (Alexander the Great).

ca. 330 B.C.   Rise of New Comedy.

322 B.C.   Aristotle dies.

317 B.C.   Menander's *Dyscolus.*

291 B.C.   Menander dies.

ca. 284–
ca. 204 B.C.   Life of Livius Andronicus, the first Roman writer.

ca. 254 B.C.   Plautus born.

241 B.C.   The First Punic War concludes.

240 B.C.   Livius Andronicus produces the first comedy at Rome.

218 B.C.	Hannibal and the Carthaginians invade Italy in the Second Punic War.
ca. 206 B.C.	Plautus' *Miles Gloriosus*.
ca. 202 B.C.	Plautus' *Cistellaria*.
202 B.C.	Scipio Africanus defeats the forces of Carthage, ending the Second Punic War.
200 B.C.	Plautus' *Stichus*.
ca. 195 B.C.	Terence born.
191 B.C.	Plautus' *Pseudolus*.
186 B.C.	The Roman Senate outlaws Dionysiac cults.
184 B.C.	Plautus dies.
166 B.C.	Terence's *Andria*.
163 B.C.	Terence's *Heauton Timorumenos*.
161 B.C.	Terence's *Eunuchus* and *Phormio*.
160 B.C.	Terence's *Hecyra* and *Adelphoe*.
159 B.C.	Terence dies.

Chapter 1

Aristophanes and the Greek Old Comedy

The Nature of Greek Old Comedy

The most characteristic feature of these festivals, both rural and urban, which took place all over Greece, was the *phallophoria*, the procession in which the phallus was carried, the symbol of creative power. In the countryside, the joyful troupe, consisting of kinsmen and bringing together the whole family, men and women, masters and slaves, marched toward the temple of Dionysus. Young girls...carried on their heads baskets containing sacrificial utensils and cakes for the offering, and also jugs filled with wine and plates of figs. The people brought along the victim, a bull. This procession was accompanied by phallic songs in honor of Phales, Dionysus' joyous and licentious companion, the phallus personified. There were also japeries of all sorts, helped along by the wearing of disguises and costumes. Festive pleasantries were exchanged, and insults were traded between the participants and the onlookers. Thus was reproduced, in a grotesque way, the mythological *thiasos*—Bacchus' band of followers, satyrs, maenads, etc. These gross japeries and *phallophoriae*,

1

singing and licentious dancing, never ceased to figure in the Attic cult in which they had an essential role. After the feast that of course followed the sacrifice, the procession returned, excited by the wine, more vigorous and more aggressive. This, properly speaking, was the *komos*.[1]

As is indicated by its very name (comedy means "*komos*-song"), this is precisely the context in which comedy originated. The Athenian Dionysiac festivals, the Greater City Dionysia (March) and the Lenaea (December), were the occasions upon which drama, both comedy and tragedy, was produced, and comedy was the direct descendent of such *komoi*. So the connection between comedy and *komos* was much more than a matter of etymology. Greek comedy was performed always and exclusively within the context of Dionysiac festivals. Technically, the theater of Dionysus was the god's temple and the actors were his priests (and, at least when a poet also functioned as an actor, so was he). A comic performance was therefore a highly specialized display of Dionysiac piety.

Dionysus was not just a Greek Bacchus, a merry god of wine and the grape. His province included drunkenness but also many other things, such as madness and ecstasy, that are transformative and, so to speak, liberate the celebrant of the burden of the normal self (thus Eleutherios, "The Liberator," was one of his cult titles). In myth and literature he is often represented as a god who works his way by disguising himself or by creating illusions to deceive others. Therefore a festival in his honor was liberating in the sense that it constituted a Greek equivalent of the Roman Saturnalia, a kind of interruption of normal reality in which usual social rules and conventions did not apply. As indicated by the above quotation, the participants in this festival were free to indulge in rowdy and licentious behavior, such as obscenity of speech and gesture (often fueled by wine), and to lose themselves in exhilarating riotousness. As in a Carnival or Mardi Gras, all the frustrating constraints of civilization were loosened. As in many such festivals the world over, part of the traditional merriment consisted of making fun of things that the celebrants were obliged to take seriously in their ordinary lives. Thus such things as restrictive social conventions and intimidating authority figures are common butts of humor on such occasions. And, since a

god with a marked affinity for disguises and illusions is obviously well qualified to serve as patron deity for the theater, there is a
certain logic in selecting Dionysiac festivals as the traditional
time of year for state-sponsored competitions in which rival
poets contended for a prize.

We can only guess at the steps by which theater grew out of
such Dionysiac celebrations. All that is known for certain is
that by the fifth century B.C. both comedy and tragedy had
evolved from such beginnings. Obviously, it is easier to imagine how drama grew out of such origins in the case of comedy
than in that of tragedy. The Greater Dionysia, in its known
form, was organized by the democratic lawmaker Cleisthenes
in about 510 B.C. Its original mimetic components were competitions in tragedy and dithyramb. A comic competition was
added in 486 B.C. We know the names of a number of poets
who worked in this form, and a fair bit about the work of some
of them, but the only surviving plays are by Aristophanes
(446–385 B.C.—his eleven extant plays were written between
425 and 388).[2] In 486 B.C. the Athenians gave official recognition to preexisting kinds of performance that in all probability
had long been associated with Dionysiac revelry, now elevated
to the level of genuine literature for the first time. This is what
Aristotle says in the *Poetics* (p. 49^{b}2) and surely he knew what
he was talking about.

In reading the above description of a *komos* and comparing it
with a comedy by Aristophanes, one can readily appreciate that
many features of the original *komos* reappear as distinctive characteristics of his plays, albeit sometimes in very transmuted
forms. This is obviously true, for example, of the feature of
Aristophanic comedy that doubtless makes the strongest impression on the first-time reader, the use of choruses costumed as
animals (birds, frogs, wasps, etc.) and other fantastic beings, such
as clouds. While the use of such exotic choruses was far from
invariable—a number of Aristophanes' plays do not have them—
they seem to have been very frequent, and the wearing of such
costumes had long been traditional for choruses associated with
the *komos*. We have a number of sixth- and early fifth-century B.C.
vase paintings showing choruses dressed in this way. The costumes worn by social clubs in Carnival and Mardi Gras celebrations present a modern analogy to this tradition.

Old Comedy, like tragedy, was therefore a form of choral drama, and plays consisted of portions spoken by individual actors alternating with portions sung with accompanying dance, chanted, or spoken by the chorus (we know very little about the use of music in comedy). One can imagine the kind of curiosity that would be stimulated in an audience: how is this strange chorus going to be employed? What would it look like? It would learn to its delight that a chorus of wasps would be employed to represent the fierce and industrious temperament of the Attic peasantry, a bird chorus to represent the carefree existence of a blissfully asocial life, a chorus of clouds to hint at the airy and nebulous teachings of the sham philosopher Socrates. We can probably assume that the chorus's costume would be suitably novel and colorful. The chorus functions as a kind of collective character. Usually, but not always, it takes the side of the play's sympathetic central character, although its allegiance is capable of shifting: in several plays (*The Acharnians*, *The Birds*, *The Wasps*) it is initially hostile to the hero but is brought over to his side as the result of his persuasive eloquence.

Three other striking Aristophanic features probably had their origins in *komos* practices. The first is the frequent use of obscenity, both verbal and visual (the phallus remains a part of comedy as a traditional appendage of the actor's costume). Even for an age of the world that is used to frank talk about sex and scatology, Aristophanes' language on these subjects can seem very strong. Any laundered translation of his plays fails to give a truthful picture of his art. It seems likely that such *komos* obscenity originally had a magical function: to confer good luck or to ward off bad. But doubtless Aristophanes was blissfully unaware of any such purpose. Often, like Rabelais or many other comedians in the Rabelaisian tradition, he revels in obscenity for the pure fun of it.

Much the same thing can be said about another prominent Aristophanic trait, a steady barrage of insults aimed at contemporary Athenians. These range from one-line "zingers" to extensive unflattering portraits of the poet's contemporaries, both famous and humble, executed in loving detail. In the original *komos*, such humor may also have had some such magical function as warding off evil spirits or ill luck by apotropaic mock-cursing, especially as obscenity and insult must often have been combined, as they frequently are in Aristophanes.

This perpetual interest in personal insult had an interesting effect. Attic comedy of all periods employed masks. In later times, these consisted of a set of stereotyped masks that came to be traditional (the romantic young man, the soubrette, the stern father, the kindly old man, and so forth). Quite possibly Old Comedy employed some stock masks too. But since Old Comedy poets often introduced living individuals as characters in their plays (think of Euripides and Socrates in Aristophanes!), this meant that special masks frequently had to be manufactured. Since comic masks were grotesque and cartoonlike exaggerations of the human face (costumes were equally distortive), when caricatures of real individuals were brought on the stage an Old Comedy must have been something like a moving and talking equivalent of a modern editorial-page cartoon.

If antiauthoritarian humor is part and parcel of such festivals, it is probably not coincidental that there is a deeply antinomian strain in Aristophanic comedy. The poet is never so happy as when he is poking fun at political leaders or other figures of high prestige in contemporary Athens, or at the cant and sacred cows of his society. In the same way, we shall see that in many of his plays the sympathetic central figure is somebody who rebels against social convention of one form or another, and so his plays are often celebrations of anti- or asocial behavior.

What these traits add up to is a remarkable freedom of speech. Although such license was already built into the *komos*, its scope was greatly enlarged. Athenian democracy prided itself on its tolerance of the freedom of each citizen to speak his mind with impunity. In this heady democratic atmosphere, comedy rapidly became politicized. The humor of personal abuse was freely deployed against prominent political figures, and the comic poets employed their freedom to speak their minds on important issues of the day. High culture and literature also became frequent comic targets. As the Athenians became increasingly caught up in intellectual interests, these too became grist for the comic mill. Aristophanes evidently had the freedom to parody and poke fun at anything imaginable, politics and religion not excluded. We hear of a series of attempts by his victims and their friends to stifle him and the other Old Comedy poets, but as long as Athenian democracy thrived in the fifth century B.C. such efforts all came to nothing.

What is more important, Old Comedy inherits the spirit of the *komos*. By this I am not speaking merely of the obvious, that Old Comedy is effervescent, joyous, extravagant, fantastic, and life-affirming. To a large extent its inner spirit and characteristic outlook are shaped by the double influence of its origins in the *komos* and its continued performance within the context of these festivals honoring Dionysus.

In an influential study of Shakespeare's comedies, C. L. Barber[3] has shown how these plays reflect the conditions and attitudes peculiar to festive holidays. A holiday is by nature an interruption of the normal round of social existence. As we have seen, usual rules of behavior and daily social distinctions are relaxed, if not abolished altogether, by a socially sanctioned suspension of constraint. This certainly was true of Dionysiac festivals, and goes a long way toward explaining why the powers that be were so opposed to the spread of the god's cult, not only in Greek mythology (memorably dramatized by Euripides in *The Bacchae*) but also when the cult spread to Republican Rome and the Senate enforced its suppression. This observation will prove not to be just an incidental remark, for it turns out that the eternal duel between the god's supporters and the god's enemies is very central to ancient comedy's outlook.

The major and most obvious reason for a holiday is to have fun. But holidays frequently perform another role as well. They serve as a mechanism for venting the aggravations, frustrations, and resentments felt by Man the animal, obliged to live a socialized existence. At times this is harmless, is in fact an approved instrument of socialization. At other times, the holiday can take on a very different tone. Barber acknowledges as much:

> When we write about holiday license as custom, our detached position is apt to result in a misleading impression that no tensions or chances are involved. For those participating, however, license is not simply a phase in a complacent evolution to foreknown conclusions; it means, at some level, disruption.[4]

This means that comedy is about fun, but also about freedom and about the testing of its limits—not without risks. On the

Aristophanic stage, the central character—let us provisionally call him the comic hero, without immediately asking about the nature of his heroism—wants the freedom to enjoy fun, the same kind of fun now being enjoyed by the holiday-making theatergoers but extended into a permanent condition, and he is willing to go to desperate lengths to gain this objective.

The typical Aristophanic hero is a reasonably average Athenian. Often the spectator is given sufficient information about the hero's social status to assure him of this. When we first meet him, he is miserable and sufficiently desperate that he will do anything to escape the situation that oppresses him. The source of his distress can be something as specific as the Peloponnesian War (as in *The Acharnians*, *Peace*), the situation in the Athenian courts (*The Wasps*), economic crisis facing the city (*Plutus*), and personal insolvency (*The Clouds*), or as vague and abstract as a generalized alienation from civilized life (*The Birds*). So, almost as an act of despair, the hero takes a bold leap into fantasy, devising a daring scheme that has the effect of standing reality on its head. When oppressed by the general malaise of life in Athens, he may decide to form a new city-state in midair, populated by birds rather than men. Or if he is troubled by the Peloponnesian War and its attendant problems, he may elect to resign from Athens, enter into a kind of asocial limbo, and strike his own private peace; alternatively, he may choose to defy the gods themselves and dig up the goddess Peace, whom they have buried, to end the War. Vexed that bad men are wealthy while good men go a-starving, he may find the blind wealth-god Plutus and cure his vision in the hope that the god will be more just when he can see what he is doing.

It is not easy for him to put his scheme into action: the forces of authority strive to block his efforts and he is obliged to struggle against them. The Aristophanic hero is typically a highly combative fellow, and a considerable amount of onstage argumentation and physical fighting supplies the plays with much of their comic energy. After his idea has been put into action, the hero is again beset by a series of antagonists. This time they are not, on the whole, representatives of established authority trying to obstruct him, but rather a string of pretentious moochers who want to take advantage of his plan for their own selfish purposes. To enjoy the fruits of his success, the hero is obliged to fend off these rascals, and when he does he manages to reveal to the audience their essential fraudulence.

At the end of the play, we see the hero triumphant, crowing in delight and hailed by one and all as a glorious victor. The play concludes with a party embracing actors, chorus, and spectators alike, as the performers toss food into the audience and Heracles' traditional victory chant is sung. Thus the play does not come to an end so much as it dissolves into its contextual background of the Dionysiac revels.

There are several points worth making about this typical pattern. First, modern writers often call the central character the "Aristophanic hero." This label raises obvious questions about the nature of his heroism. Certainly he is heroic in the sense that he is obliged to enter into a series of combats and contentions to achieve his goal. Sometimes, but not always, his quest is not undertaken exclusively on his own behalf, so that some group (friends, fellow Attic farmers, all morally upright men, even the entire city) benefits from his success. In such situations he is heroic precisely in the sense that heroes like monster-killing Heracles are, since his fellow men profit from his victories. But he is also a hero in the sense that, as an average Athenian, he is someone with whom the typical spectator can readily identify. He is the irrepressible "little man" who refuses to be intimidated by all the things that would very much cow his real-life equivalent. But there is nothing Chaplinesque about him. The Aristophanic hero is bold and pugnacious; he is never pathetic and we are never invited to feel sorry for him. And often he has an amusing mean streak. In the end he manages to turn the tables on an overwhelming and oppressive world and emerge triumphant. He is a character daring and fortunate enough to translate the average spectator's fantasies of achieving fun and freedom into bold action. He also enacts the kind of fantasies of empowerment and omnipotence studied by Alfred Adler, and it is worth bearing in mind that Adler was primarily a criminologist concerned with fantasies associated with antisocial behavior.

These considerations make clear what otherwise would be puzzling: the way our sympathies are oriented once we have entered the world of comedy. They are always firmly on the side of the comic hero and his enterprises. And, since he is constantly required to enter into fights with people who either want to keep him from achieving his goals or to take unfair advantage of his successes, we regard all of his opponents and rivals as the comic equivalent of villains. We are of course encouraged to regard them as villains by the highly unflattering light in which they are all portrayed, as unfeeling, grotesque, selfish, hypocritical, comically ineffectual, etc. The spectator is encouraged to realize that they are all hypocrites in the sense that there is a visible disparity between what they are and what they ought to be or claim to be. The spectator's sympathies are thus oriented essentially because the hero's ultimate aim is to have the freedom to enjoy life, and so his antagonists are portrayed as antifun and antifreedom. Translated into other terms, the hero is attuned to Dionysus, and his antagonists are therefore cast as the comic equivalents of the dour and repressive opponent of the god (in comic criticism such a figure is sometimes called an "agelast"—a man who does not know how to laugh and who therefore tries to spoil the fun of others).

Tragedy as well as comedy was performed as a gesture of Dionysiac piety. Although most tragedies had "nothing to do with Dionysus," at the end of his career Euripides revived a kind of tragedy that otherwise flourished only near the time of tragedy's beginning. The Bacchae (ca. 406 B.C.) tells the story of how Dionysus, accompanied by his attendant rout of maenads, appears at Thebes and insistently demands recognition. Pentheus, the king, refuses to acknowledge that Dionysus is a god, separating him from his retinue. Two wiser old men of the community, Cadmus and Teiresias, recognize the god's authenticity and participate in his worship. They try to talk some reason into Pentheus' head, but he stubbornly refuses to heed them. Finally he is hideously destroyed by the god's followers. The god triumphs, his power and reality now thoroughly acknowledged, and his followers can be reunited with their master.

Although most tragedies did not have to do with Dionysiac myths, they were followed by short farcical afterpieces called satyr plays because their choruses were invariably composed of goatlike satyrs who, like the maenads, were traditional members of Dionysus' retinue. The single completely surviving example of a satyr play is Euripides' Cyclops. This is a comic retelling of the well-known story of Odysseus and the Cyclops, first told in

Homer's *Odyssey*, and seems to be a typical representative of its genre. Euripides represents the satyrs as having become separated from Dionysus. Therefore Odysseus' defeat of the horrible ogre permits their reunion with the god.

And here, we may note in passing, is the apparent answer to a problem that puzzled us earlier: how could dramatic forms as different as tragedy and comedy both grow out of the same joyous Dionysiac *komos*? Scholars often regard *The Bacchae* as a throwback to a very primitive kind of tragedy, and so it looks significant that both this type of tragedy and comedy dramatize the same essential plot. Dionysus' opponents refuse to recognize the god, and so their defeat involves a reaffirmation of his power and authenticity. Because the production of any kind of play was a gesture of Dionysiac piety, this reaffirmation was an essential purpose of any kind of drama. As tragedy continued to evolve, however, playwrights turned to other kinds of subject matter and dramatized episodes from the great fund of Greek heroic myth. But when this change occurred, toward the end of the sixth century B.C., conservatives loudly complained that the newfangled kind of tragedy had nothing to do with Dionysus.

At bottom, both *The Bacchae* and *Cyclops* (and of course a number of other items of specifically Dionysiac literature)[5] contain variants of this same plot, which therefore may be called the *hieros logos*, or official sacred myth of the god's cult. In both plays, Dionysus' followers have become separated from the god. Their very single-minded goal is to become reunited with him, to regain a lost wholeness. Standing in their way is the villain of the piece, who both separates them from Dionysus and denies the god's power and authenticity. His defeat is necessary to create the conditions under which the followers can rejoin Dionysus. In this sense, therefore, an agelast can be redefined as someone who stands between Dionysus and his followers, separating them against their will.

But it is not enough to defeat the god's antagonist. A strong element of humiliation must also be present. Before being ripped apart by the maenads, Pentheus is tricked by the god's illusions into dressing as a woman and walking through the city, a butt of mockery. Odysseus and the satyrs jeer at the blinded Polyphemus.

So Pentheus may be described as a tragic agelast. He is as impervious to the reality of Dionysus and what he represents in life as a tone-deaf man is to a symphony, and so he actively sets himself up as the god's opponent. Or you could put the matter differently. The comic figure of the fun-spoiling agelast is comedy's equivalent of the tragic figure Pentheus. In either case, the same story is being retold, be it in tragic or comic terms.

If the comic hero is to achieve his ambitions of freedom and fun, he must first inflict a decisive defeat on his agelastic opponents. Such a defeat is always marked by a strong element of humiliation, in that the agelast is made the audience's laughing-stock as all his pretensions are stripped away and his hypocrisy (the disparity between what he claims to be and what he is) is revealed. In a dramatic form enacted as an act of piety toward Dionysus, the spectator is strongly invited to sympathize with the comic hero precisely because he is in tune with the god's program of merrymaking, and so regard agelasts as the comic equivalent of villains.

If you pause to think about it, the results of this orientation can be very curious. If the comic hero's motivations and activities were to be regarded in the dispassionate light of everyday reality, they would sometimes look very different. For the Aristophanic hero's enterprise is often asocial, antisocial, or downright criminal, and his motivations are sometimes spectacularly selfish. One of the seeming puzzles of Aristophanic comedy—and of much comedy written ever since—is that on the comic stage we are encouraged to tolerate or even applaud activities and motives that in real life we would, or at least should, find deplorable. Likewise, some of the hero's antagonists do not look very different from the hero himself. Certainly in the case of Aristophanes' more selfish heroes, the self-serving motives of the parasites who want to batten onto the success of his venture cannot be the differentiating consideration that makes us like him and applaud when he subjects them to discomfiture and humiliation.

In a Dionysiac and comic context, considerations of fun and freedom are so predominant that they override any others, including those of morality. Our sympathies are planted so firmly on the side of the fun-seeker that we see anything and anybody standing in his way in an unsympathetic light.

11

Additionally, of course, part of the fun both of comedy and of the holiday festival in which it is enacted consists of being able to thumb your nose at all sorts of things that you are obliged to take seriously in the everyday world: frequent targets are social conformity and its agents, including parents. Conventional morality is not exempted from such disrespectful handling.

And here is the real difference between Old Comedy and the other great dramatic form that flourished at the same time, Attic tragedy. Tragedy is a highly moralizing genre.[6] Comedy, as we shall see in the course of this study, can be moralistic too, but it can also be surprisingly amoral. Take that most central of moral problems, hubris. Many tragedies are, among other things, morality plays showing the folly of hubristic disrespect toward, or rebellion against, the gods. But some comedies (Aristophanes' *The Birds* and *Plutus* spring to mind) show a comic hero whose enterprise is precisely hubristic, without calling his activities or attitudes into question. Rather, Aristophanic comedy regularly celebrates rugged individualism carried to extremes, unchecked by any conventions of socialization, morality, or piety. Aristophanes was well aware of this fundamental tension between comedy and tragedy, and he spends a great deal of time parodying specific tragedies and poking fun at individual tragic poets. The cumulative effect of all this humor is the cultivation of a disrespectful attitude toward tragedy in general. (No such tension could exist between later Greek comedy and tragedy, because after the fifth century B.C. Attic tragedy became fossilized and was no longer a vital art form).

The alignment of the spectator's sympathies is encouraged by the fact that fun-seeking comic heroes and their friends are regularly presented as bright, original, clever, dynamic, and healthy. But those who cannot become attuned to Dionysus are variously portrayed as stodgy, dull, grotesque, hypocritical, or somehow morbid or unpleasant. By every conceivable means, the spectator is encouraged to laugh with the sympathetic characters and to cheer their successes. Likewise, he is encouraged to laugh at the unsympathetic characters and take pleasure in the defeats and humiliations they suffer. In traditional comedy, the spectator is scarcely encouraged to make a more critical or thoughtful evaluation of comic characters. Thus, for example, there is no demand that the spectator pass any kind of moral judgment on the comic hero's selfishness. In the last chapter of this study we shall see that Terence revolutionized the nature of ancient comedy by taking a more penetrating and realistic look at his characters and the traits they embody.

Since Aristophanic comedy is, among other things, political comedy written by a poet capable of using humor to make points meant seriously, such derision of established norms, institutions, social authority, and the individuals who represent these things can at times acquire a more pointed effect. Comic derision can be aimed at other things that can intimidate the average citizen: for example, the highfalutin world of high art or intellectualism, both of which have pretensions to their own kind of cultural authority. When authority of any form, and the kinds of people who represent it, are comically explored and shown to be unpleasant, grotesque, hypocritically self-centered, and above all when they are shown to be impotent—as they always are when the hero humiliates and defeats them—the effect is strongly debunking. The audience is invited to dislike and disdain them and, since there is no watertight bulkhead between the world of the festival and that of everyday life, there is a serious attempt to instruct the spectator's feelings on the matter at hand.

All the generalizations made so far about Aristophanes' comic heroes have been couched exclusively in masculine terms. In two Aristophanic plays the central character is a woman (the title role in the *Lysistrata*, Praxagora in *The Ecclesiazusae*), but Aristophanes' comic heroines seem constructed according to a different psychological model. They are less selfish, less interested in their own fun, and more concerned about the community's welfare rather than their own. Nevertheless his heroines have certain traits in common with his central male characters: Lysistrata and Praxagora are also rebels against society who invert its conventions for their own purposes.

Aristophanes does not always adhere to the plot outline I have described, but it appears in enough of his plays (*The Acharanians*, *Peace*, *The Birds*, *Plutus*, and *The Wasps* in a somewhat modified form) that it can fairly be described as his regular format. Other plays deviate from this plan to a greater or lesser extent, and present us with different kinds of central characters, but in all the plays the inner spirit remains the same: strongly pro-fun, pro-freedom, and in consequence perpetually antinomian and disrespectful of authority. An important component of this study's central thesis, used as a kind of baseline, is that one of the ways in which ancient comedy presents us with a continuum is that all ancient comedies, Greek as well as Roman, were performed at festivals. The Greek New Comedy continued to be performed at the Dionysia and the Lenaea, and Roman comedy was performed at various Roman holidays (*ludi*). This is more than historical coincidence. Ancient comedies were uniformly produced in this holiday context and consequently are imbued with the spirit of the festival holiday.

Later Greek and Byzantine dramatic historians divided Greek comedy into three historical phases: the Old, Middle, and New Comedies. Modern writers have generally inherited the habit of looking at ancient comedy as a series of individual phases, each tied to a distinct historical epoch and a different set of social conditions. But in the sense that all ancient comedy is festive comedy we are entitled to speak of Greco-Roman comedy as a unified dramatic tradition.

This is not to deny the obvious fact that over the centuries Roman comedy has had a much greater impact on our later comic tradition than has Aristophanes. Via the *commedia dell'arte* many of the standard character types and plot moves of New and Roman comedy were conveyed to the Renaissance. Appearing in the comedies of such writers as Shakespeare and Moliére, they became stock elements of modern Western comedy, including comic opera and the comic novel and film. It is very difficult to start listing specific examples, because once one begins it would be impossible to stop. Suffice it to say that our comic tradition is permeated with elements inherited from later antiquity, and the reader familiar with these elements will spot them constantly resurfacing in a host of contemporary guises.

But some of the important ingredients of the Western comic formula had not yet been invented in Aristophanes' day. For example, much later comedy revolves around situations of mistaken identity or misunderstood motives, but no Aristophanic play makes important use of these devices. Then too, the single most important kind of fun-seeking in New and Roman comedy consists of a young man struggling for the freedom to enjoy his darling by overcoming the obstacles to true love, so that one of these plays typically ends with a marriage or reunion of lovers. Aristophanes and his contemporaries seem to have been entirely uninterested in boy-meets-girl stories. Likewise, much of the comic effect in later comedy is created by artfully constructed plots. Aristophanes was not exactly a master of plotting, at least as plotting was later understood by Aristotle and other literary critics. In terms of structure, in comparison with later classical comedy his plays might strike a modern reader as very ram-shackle, episodic affairs. The idea that the comic effect, no less than the tragic one, could best be achieved by tight and effective plotting had not yet occurred. All three of these comic discover-ies remained to be made by the playwrights of the New Comedy. But on the most basic level of all, that of informative spirit and characteristic, innate outlook, the comic continuum does exist and can be traced to the spirit and outlook of the Dionysia.

But the thesis that we can speak of such a continuum in ancient comedy does not rest on this single point. The subject matter of most Greek tragedies consists of power struggles with-in families, and it would be worthwhile to catalogue all the vari-ous kinds of familial power struggles that the tragedians portray (brother-brother, mother-daughter, stepmother-stepchild, etc.). Comedy also deals with such power struggles, occasionally in Aristophanes and much more regularly thereafter. But, unlike tragedy, ancient comedy takes a particular interest in one form of contention within the family, contests between sons and their fathers.

The situation of the fun-seeking young man finding himself thwarted by his father is a common one in a dramatic form that perennially pits the fun-seeking individual against his repressive surrounding society. The father, after all, is the immediate repre-sentative of social authority within the family. Fathers can thus be cast in the role of antagonists who need to be overcome, and can be given a characterization that is negative or somehow com-ically unpleasant. New and Roman comedies dramatize this nuclear plot situation frequently.

More generally, in comedies as different as Aristophanes' *The Wasps* (where the situation is handled by inversion) and Plautus' *Mostellaria*, we see the *dramatis personae* of a play divided into two warring camps, those constellated around the son, who are on the side of freedom and fun, and those enucleated around the father, opposed to these principles. But this latter camp, collectively representing the older generation, sometimes has a traitor in its midst: a man old in years but still young at heart, who is still capable of having his fun, and so is in effect the ally of the younger generation since he shares its attitudes and outlook. Then again, in the world of comedy it is the invariable rule that the young at heart and the fun-loving must ultimately prevail. Sometimes they do so by inflicting an outright defeat on those who would stand in their way. At other times, the climactic reversal is more interesting: rather than merely being overcome or outwitted, an agelastic father or similarly dour old man undergoes a kind of Dionysiac conversion that, like its Christian counterpart, involves a genuine rebirth or restructuring of his personality. Thus, looking at things from this character's point of view, the ultimate effect of the play is to shift him from one camp to the other.

That Aristophanes was well aware of the underlying geometry of son-father confrontations can be seen from a short episode in *The Birds*. Peisthetairus has founded Cloudcuckooland, and a steady queue of parasites, frauds, and get-rich-quick artists comes parading across the stage, trying to claim an unwarranted share of his success. But he quickly penetrates the sham of each, and dismisses them all derisively with much verbal and physical abuse. Interspersed among these bogus claimants is a young man (1337–71) who has heard the glad news that Peisthetairus' new city-state is such an anarchic place that a son can commit violence against his father. His simple ambition is to strangle his dad and inherit the family property.

The striking feature of this passage is the remarkable way in which he is treated by Peisthetairus. He is sent packing, but with none of the humiliating abuse meted out to the other postulants in this scene. There is something instructively tolerant and understanding in Peisthetairus' reaction to the young man's ambition.

Father-son contention plays a more central role in the two plays to which we now turn, *The Wasps* and *The Clouds*. Both of these plays operate on two levels. The former takes a comic look at the Attic courts, as presided over by the demagogues who governed Athens during the Peloponnesian War. *The Clouds* examines the new education offered by the sophists represented, rather unfairly, by Socrates. But on another level both deal with the father-son relationship, and it is this second level with which we shall primarily be concerned.

Neither play dramatizes the situation of a fun-seeking son striving to overcome a repressive father. Rather, this archetypal pattern is hilariously manipulated. Thus in *The Wasps* a fine effect is created by inverting the normal situation and showing a fun-seeking father struggling to achieve freedom from the control of his dourly repressive son. In *The Clouds* we see another secondary elaboration on the pattern. For his own disreputable purposes a father encourages his son to enlarge on his fun-loving to the point that, like a comic Frankenstein, he creates a monster. Then, of course, comedy's equivalent of poetic justice is executed when he becomes the monster's first victim. But neither plot would produce the desired comic effect if there were no recognizable underlying pattern to be manipulated.

The Wasps

The play opens with two slaves keeping a night watch: one of them rather mysteriously alludes to some beast they are guarding. They try to sleep but are immediately awoken by nightmares. One of them has had a particularly bad one: he dreamt of a flock of sheep sitting down in the Pnyx with their little cloaks. Then a greedy grampus made a speech to them, squealing like a scalded pig. The dream is easy to decipher, as the other slave perceives: it signifies the vile demagogue Cleon making a speech to the sheeplike Athenian people.

One of the slaves turns to the audience and addresses it directly (54ff.). Don't expect any of the usual nugatory stuff; there'll be no attacks against Euripides or Cleon. We have something completely different for you. You see this house here? The man sleeping up on the roof is our master and he is, with our help, keeping his father locked within. For the old fellow suffers from a strange disease, of an entirely unpredictable nature. Then they play a little guessing game. No, he is not a dice-lover, a drink-lover, or anything you would expect. He is a courtroom-lover. He has a complete mania for trials, and is utterly devastated whenever he cannot serve on a jury. Even in his dreams he goes back to the courtroom, and his hand is frozen into a claw from holding the pebbles with which Athenian jurymen cast their votes. First thing in the morning, he dashes to the court and finishes his sleep while waiting for admittance. This makes him so irritable that he always hands in a vote of "guilty." He even keeps a pebble-beach at home so that he will have a stock of voting-stones.

Recognizing this mania for the disease it is, his son has attempted all the standard cures for madness to no good effect. The father just kept zipping back to the courtroom. Try to lock him in the house and out he goes over the roof, or he drives pegs in the wall and climbs down. So they have had to spread nets over the building to keep him pent up within. The old man's name is Philocleon ("Cleon-Lover") and the son's is Bdelycleon ("Cleon-Hater").

Bdelycleon wakes up and chides the slaves for neglecting their duty. He has the idea that his father has gotten into the kitchen and may be trying to escape through the drain. But he is interrupted by a scraping noise in the chimney. He sees somebody emerging from it and asks him who he is. "I'm smoke" is the reply. He is of course Philocleon, and is shoved back into the chimney. But all of a sudden he is at the door, chewing at the lock. When this fails he tries to gnaw through the net, and Bdelycleon is obliged to remind him that he has no teeth left. Next a donkey appears, with the old man clinging to its belly in a parody of Odysseus' method of escape from the Cyclops' cave. When this attempt is foiled Bdelycleon and the slaves relock the door and pile a heap of rocks in front of it (proper way of dealing with a pseudo-Odysseus) and Philocleon pops up on the roof. But he is safely restrained within the house.

All this is very funny, and would be funnier still if we could see it on the stage with Philocleon played by a physically gifted actor. For Philocleon, with his great demonic energy, is the most physically demanding role in the Aristophanic repertoire. But this scene also raises severe questions. The Athenians regarded the situation of a son committing violence against his father with extreme distaste. And yet this is precisely what is happening here, with nobody (including Philocleon, at least in so many words) challenging his right to do so. And throughout the play it is made abundantly clear that Bdelycleon has control over the family purse strings and property, which he may dole out to his father as he wishes. So it looks as if Bdelycleon has displaced his father as head of the household. How can this be?

Mention is made of Philocleon's strange form of insanity, but nowhere in the play are we given an explicit diagnosis of his problem. Probably the Athenian audience would have understood the situation in terms that Aristophanes does not spell out. There was a provision in Attic law that if the head of a household became mentally incompetent, his son could obtain a special writ displacing him and transferring familial authority to himself. The father was thus placed in a legally sanctioned wardship.

As the play progresses it becomes increasingly obvious that Philocleon's problem is senility. Senility is notoriously a kind of second childhood—Aristophanes says so at *The Clouds* 1417—and everything about Philocleon is calculated to seem childlike. Like a child, he is spontaneous and terrifically vigorous. But also, like a child, he is willful, ever insistent on instant gratification, petulant, and given to tantrums. Even his startling amorality has an infantile quality to it.

In real life, a parent's senility is a domestic tragedy, but a tragedy that can have the peculiar quality of creating hilarious incidents that become the stuff of family legend. On the comic stage, Aristophanes can skip the tragic aspects and focus on the humor to be extracted from the situation. On one level *The Wasps* is a comic look at abuses current in Athens's court systems and another hit against Aristophanes' political enemies. But throughout the play a second level of humor is at work that consists of a reversal of normal family role-stereotyping. If Philocleon is the willful child, this has the effect of casting Bdelycleon in the role of the restrictive parent. If the normal situation is for a child to want to slip out from under his parent's authority to have his fun, here the situation is inverted and the play could just as well have a subtitle borrowed from a long-defunct comic strip, *Bringing Up Father*. This level of humor is operative in a number of scenes, and some critics have unjustly complained about the alleged irrelevance of the play's conclusion, in which Philocleon finally breaks loose and defeats much younger men in an impromptu dancing contest, because they have failed to appreciate that it constitutes a kind of working-out of this subplot.

The Wasps is a lampoon of the ultra-democrat Cleon and the way he has gained power over the court system. He and his cronies have control of the doling out of jurors' salaries. There is now living in Athens a sort of wartime proletariat consisting of ruined Attic farmers obliged to take refuge in the city. The chorus of highly waspish Attic peasants are drawn from this class. Unemployed farmers form the bulk of jurymen, and consequently jurors are dependent on the demagogues for their daily bread. Worse yet, in the supercharged atmosphere of wartime, charges of treason are hurled about very lightly, and so the demagogues can haul their political opponents before suborned juries and have them condemned for no good reason.

All of which Bdelycleon patiently explains to Philocleon in an attempt to wean him away from his courtroom-madness, and so Aristophanes' initial promise not to make fun of Cleon is of course broken. But here we are less interested in the public and political level of comedy in the play than in the domestic interaction of father and son.

In some other plays Aristophanes gives some surprisingly particular information about how his characters are located in Athenian society. Such is the case, for example, in *The Clouds*, in which we are informed about Strepsiades' rural background and the specific countryside district from which he came; his wife's pedigree is even grafted onto the genealogy of a very prominent Athenian family to which Pericles himself, the great statesman of Attic democracy, had belonged. We are provided with no such explicit facts about Philocleon's background, but some inferences can be made. The chorus, full of peasant grumbles and concerns, comes to his house and tries to call him out. Although his household evidently enjoys reasonable prosperity, they clearly regard him as one of their own and so we may probably deduce that Philocleon is an ex-farmer who for some unspecified reason has moved to the city. Certainly, as the play unfolds he displays some very peasantlike traits. Bdelycleon, in comparison, is much more urbane and sophisticated. City ways have seemingly rubbed off on him in a way they have not on his father.

During his meeting with the chorus Philocleon makes a candid admission. When explaining that his son has locked him up, he complains that his son "will not let me sit on a jury or work any harm" (340). This confession proves to be important, as throughout the play his uncomplicated inner motivation is quite simply to hurt people. He makes further frantic attempts at escape, with the chorus cheering him on, and when Bdelycleon shows up to restrain him the chorus rounds on him as a traitor bent on installing tyranny in Athens. This leads to a debate in front of the chorus, in which Philocleon seeks to prove that he and his fellow judges are lords of the universe. Philocleon brags of how defendants are forced to grovel before juries, pandering to their every whim, and how much fun it is for jurors to humiliate them. So do their families, since jurors are breadwinners (at 606ff. he volunteers a remarkable description of how each night his daughter is obliged to fish his juryman's salary out of his mouth with her tongue). He is so intoxicated with this power that he goes so far as to claim (619ff.) that his dominion is no less powerful than Zeus' own.

Bdelycleon refutes all this bluster with a demonstration that jurors are actually Cleon's abject slaves. Philocleon is utterly shattered by this rebuttal. He has previously promised to fall on his sword if he were to be worsted in the debate, but now he is so unmanned that he cannot even carry out this promise (713ff.). There is something childish about his dramatic mood swing, as he plummets from the heights of prideful arrogance to the depths of confusion and despair. Therefore he readily yields to Bdelycleon's injunction that he forswear the law courts and allow his son to provide him with a life of domestic ease. He will be provided with all an old man's necessities: gruel to slurp, comfortable clothes, a blanket, a girl to masturbate him (715ff.).

But even in his devastated condition Philocleon cannot bear to part with the beloved pleasures of the courtroom. Bdelycleon has a bright idea. He will establish a court at home and Philocleon can play the juryman here, imposing fines on delinquent servants. And so a domestic trial is enacted, in which Labes the dog is put on trial for stealing a Sicilian cheese from the kitchen, while Bdelycleon plays variously the parts of bailiff, prosecutor, and defendant's advocate, and various kitchen implements are introduced as witnesses. Although part of the humor of this scene was political (it has to do with the peculations of a general named Laches during his campaigning in Sicily), this episode is also funny just as a burlesque trial, and because this reminds one of a domestic entertainment parents might stage for the amusement of a child. The kind of visual humor that permeates this scene—the dog and the testifying utensils must have been represented on stage by extras wearing bizarre costumes—would have great appeal for children. Certainly Philocleon acts like a thoroughly spoiled child throughout the scene, as he is imperious, fussy, and insistent on being the center of attention.

At the end of this trial Philocleon is tricked into voting to acquit the dog. Again he is crushed: as a juror, the height of his pleasure was to hand in a guilty vote, no matter what.

So the old man's enthusiasm for the law courts is undone entirely. Bdelycleon tries a new tack, by transforming his father into a citified gentleman. There is an amusing scene (1122ff.) in which he tries to make him dress as an upper-class Athenian and to teach him the proper etiquette for dignified parties. Throughout the scene the old man plays stupid and refuses to absorb this urbane lore. Here we seem to be shown a peasant resisting any attempt at citification. But again, this is a kind of a reversal of a normal parent's effort to socialize a child and teach him proper manners.

Philocleon is sent off to such a high-class party, and the results are predictably disastrous. A household slave staggers in (1292ff.) describing the old man's riotous behavior. He got drunk, behaved outrageously, and managed to insult each and every fellow guest in turn. Then he headed homeward, physically attacking anybody he met in the street. Obviously there is a kind of comic displacement going on here. Once Philocleon had his fun by doing wrong and harming people in the courts. Now that this avenue has been closed, his impulse to hurt his fellow man has merely found a different and more direct outlet. The fact that the one method was legally acceptable and the second is not counts for nothing.

This latter insight is suggested by the fact that as soon as the reeling Philocleon comes on stage (1326) some of his assault-and-battery victims now show up demanding justice and threatening lawsuits. His response is remarkable:

Hoo boy, you're suing me! How old-fashioned of you! Don't you know that I can't stand to hear about lawsuits? Hee hee, this is my pleasure. The hell with your ballot boxes! (1335ff.)

As more of his victims collect on stage, he fends them off with violent verbal and physical abuse. His reaction to their repeated threats of lawsuits is one of deep disinterest. So, in one sense, his personality has been transformed, although in another it has not. There is a psychoanalytic doctrine that if you manage to deprive a neurotic of his symptoms without eliminating the neurosis itself, he will merely develop new ones. Exactly the same has happened here. Bdelycleon's wish has been fulfilled in that Philocleon has been cured of his courtroom-mania. But the cure proves worse than the disease. The new Philocleon is just as unmanageably rambunctious as ever but, since his new mode of operation is to inflict direct physical harm on people, he has become more problematic than ever. In both *The Wasps* and, as we shall see, *The Clouds*, there is a climactic comic reversal whereby someone's plan succeeds, but with unexpected disastrous results.

At the party Philocleon has acquired a courtesan, whom he has brought home. He now addresses her, and part of his speech is worth quoting:

> When my son dies I shall buy your freedom and keep you as a play-mate, my little porker. Now I have no control over my own affairs. For I am young and kept under careful guard. My little son keeps his eye on me, that grouchy, cumin-chopping-mustard-grinding man, and he is afraid lest I go to perdition. But he's the only father I have. (1351ff.)

This is interesting as providing some confirmation of our initial suspicions that Bdelycleon has had his father certified as senile and keeps him in wardship. It also renders explicit the comic dynamic that has driven the play from the beginning, the reversal of generational roles. Even more pointed is the first sentence of the quotation. When we turn to Roman Comedy we shall repeatedly encounter the situation of a son hoping for his father's death so that inherited money will allow him to fulfill his amorous ambitions. Here this comic son's perennial wish is inverted (and, one wonders, how could this strike an audience as funny if the comic stereotype had not already been established?)

When Bdelycleon sees Philocleon with the courtesan, he is thoroughly disgusted, and repeatedly points out to the old man that her acquisition is stupid because he suffers from senile impotence (1365, 1380f.). The two men exit the stage, leaving the chorus alone to sing a song praising Bdelycleon for getting the better of his father (1450ff.). But congratulations prove to be a bit premature. For in a final scene Philocleon does manage, at last, to break free of the house in which he is restrained. A distraught slave informs the audience that he has again gotten drunk and is intent on cavorting throughout the night, dancing "those old-fashioned dances such as Thespis employed in the tragedy-competition, and he claims he'll show that your contemporary tragedians are old coots" (1478). When the old man comes onstage, he indeed is performing those energetic, high-kicking dances of old, and he is doing so with amazing vigor. He issues a challenge: if any modern "tragedian"—here the word probably means "tragic actor," although of course some tragic poets also functioned as actors—thinks he can do as well, let him get up on the stage. In response to his challenge, the contemporary tragedian Carcinus and his three sons enter. In honor of the fact that Carcinus means "crab," they are evidently wearing crab costumes. The play ends with all the actors dancing, spinning, spinning on through the night.

This concluding scene has troubled commentators because it does not appear very germane to the play as a whole. However, this ending may be irrelevant to the main business of poking fun at the contemporary courts, but it is scarcely irrelevant to the second, domestic level. The real purpose of the final scene is enunciated by the slave when he says that Philocleon's boast is that he will show that the culture of earlier times is in fact younger than that of the present. For the play is shot through with old–young imagery. Philocleon is an old man. But, paradoxically, in a number of ways he is youthful, indeed more childlike than his son. Although this is partially due to senescence, in his old age he is scarcely as impotent as his son prefers to believe.

There is much more to his youthfulness than mere senility. As a man old in years but young at heart, he is, in his own peculiar way, fun-loving. Translated into the terms suggested by comedy's surrounding context, he is a man who is preeminently in touch with Dionysus. And this is not just because he is a drinking man. In Euripides' *The Bacchae* we are shown two men, Teiresias and Cadmus, who are advanced in years but neverthe-

less are determined to catch the proper spirit of a Dionysiac celebration and go out on the mountain to join the bacchic revelers.
This, from the god's viewpoint, is how people of all ages should
be: no matter how old you are, you are supposed to remain
inwardly young and fun-loving, and you are never exempt from
the god's imperious demands. For all his many and manifest
shortcomings, Philocleon is essentially in the right because, like
Teiresias and Cadmus, he heeds this imperative. His son, con-
trariwise, is cast in the unsympathetic role of a fun-spoiling agelast. In this sense, he is represented as a comic equivalent of
Pentheus.

Viewed in retrospect, *The Wasps* can be seen as a protracted
duel of wits between father and son. Bdelycleon is always, in one
way or another, seeking to restrain or reform his rambunctious
father, and the plot consists of a series of skirmishes between the
two. Philocleon may be a senescent old rascal, but he is full of life
and energy. His ideas of fun may be deplorable, but he is bent on
having his fun, and this has the effect of aligning Bdelycleon on
the side of social restraint and respectability. Bdelycleon is by no
means characterized as pathologically stuffy or inhibited and, if
he could speak, he might well care to protest the unfairness of
the position in which circumstances have placed him. Nevertheless, the dynamics of the situation cast him in a decidedly antifun
role, therefore as an obstacle that must be overcome. He manages to win some of these skirmishes, but in the end Philocleon
triumphs over his son by remaining true to his own nature and
getting his way untrammeled, and the dynamics of the situation
determine our response: we react to his triumph with pleasure
and relief.

Philocleon is perhaps the most remarkable figure in
Aristophanes' gallery of characters. With his unabashed selfishness and enthusiasm for hurting people for the pure hell of it,
this senescent incorrigible ought to strike us as appalling and
pathetic. But of course he does not, any more than does Falstaff.
A leading Aristophanist had the candor to confess:

> Recent commentators have remarked on the sympathy and affection
> which [Philocleon] evokes in the spectator and the reader. I admit
> that he evokes mine; and yet I remain astonished at the hidden
> strength of antinomian sentiment which that sympathy and affection
> imply.[7]

Philocleon is an excellent example of comedy's ability to override the sort of moral judgment that comes into play in everyday life. His case is instructive because he is a comic hero devoid of any admirable qualities whatsoever—save for those which qualify him for admirable hero-hood. Since comedy casts a complacent eye on rascality, he seems more of a lovable buffoon than a genuine menace. When he resists Bdelycleon's attempts to stop his outrageous behavior, he is engaged in a struggle to assert his continued existence as a free spirit. For if the son were to prove successful in taming him, this victory would involve a kind of mutilation of the father's selfhood and authenticity. So in the spirit of comedy we find that, despite our awareness of his many shortcomings, we are relieved that he emerges so magnificently unscathed. By remaining unchanged, he scores a moral victory over the forces of propriety. His essential object is to gain the freedom to have fun, and in accordance with the festive spirit of the Dionysia, comedy is firmly on the side of the fun-loving. Therefore his enterprises, no matter how dubious they may be, have the redeeming merit of carrying out the festival's essential program.

The Clouds

Strepsiades, a native of the rural Attic district of Cicynna, has moved into Athens and married a high-class city woman. He misses the countryside and has difficulty adapting to his wife's urbane ways, including her urbane sexual proclivities. They have produced a son, Pheidippides. The boy has inherited aristocratic tastes from his mother's side of the family and (as his equine name suggests, since it is a compound containing *hippos* as one of its elements) is horse-mad. In his mania for horses the boy has run up huge debts, and his father cannot pay off the creditors.

Worried by this huge problem, and also chewed by bedbugs, Strepsiades tosses and turns in bed, unable to sleep, wishing he were back in the country. In the small hours, he has invented a plan for salvation: he will go to the Thinking-Shop, inhabited by wise men who know all sorts of recondite lore. This is a strange shabby crew of pale-faced, barefoot men, presided over by Socrates and his lieutenant Chaerephon. If you pay them enough, they will teach you to make justice seem injustice and *vice versa*. He will become a Thinking-Shop student where, although he is a dull and forgetful old man, he can learn debt-avoiding tricks.

Without ado—scene shifts can be very fluid on the Aristophanic stage—we are transported from Strepsiades' bedroom to the front door of the Thinking-Shop. The old man is greeted by an extremely supercilious student, who reacts to his appearance with annoyance because the interruption has caused a brilliant thought to "miscarry" (136)—this may be one of the very few indisputable Socratic touches in the play, since Socrates used to compare himself to a midwife. The thought in question was a patented Thinking-Shop "mystery": Socrates was asking Chaerephon how many feet a flea could hop, when the flea bit Chaerephon's eyebrow and then jumped onto his own bald head. Then they completed the experiment by catching the flea and doing some business with melted wax. Then Strepsiades is treated to some further pseudoscience about whether gnats hum from their mouths or their rectums. And, by the way, last night Socrates was gazing upwards to study the moon—when a lizard crapped in his eye (171ff.). But Socrates devised a brilliant countermove: the Thinking-Shop crew was too poor to eat, so Socrates took a roasting-spit, bent it into a geometrician's compass, and hooked a cloak from the gymnasium next door so that they could sell it for food. Strepsiades sees some other students with their rumps sticking into the air. He learns that they are not rooting for truffles, as he had supposed, but are studying the things below the ground.

Thus we see an amusing representation of useless and nugatory scientific investigation combined with a portrait of these seedy sham-intellectuals. After a little more funny business, Socrates appears—hovering aloft in midair in a basket. This entrance, which uses the same stage machinery employed for the tragic *deus ex machina*, is visually impressive. But it is also a fine visual metaphor for Socrates' condition: impractical, "above himself," out of touch with reality. He proclaims that he hovers in midair the better to carry out his astronomical studies. Also, suspended in the kindred ether, his thoughts may roam freely and their essences will not be dragged down to earth. Then he rather spoils the pretentious effect by adding the mysterious *non sequitur* that "the very same thing happens to watercress" (234).

Strepsiades is impressed, and he gets down to business. He explains his problem and asks for help. But he makes the mistake of swearing by the gods that he will pay for debt-avoiding lessons. Socrates pounces on this. In the Thinking-Shop the traditional Greek gods are no longer worshipped. Rather, the so-called thinkers worship such strange new beings as boundless Air, bright Ether, and those great goddesses, the Clouds (263ff.). In fact, says Socrates, if you want, you may see them right now. He launches into an impressive invocation.

This is the cue for the chorus' entrance (274–363). Many Old Comedies have had animal choruses. But clouds were something entirely new and different. If the reader wonders why Aristophanes thought a cloud-chorus was appropriate for the play, he ought to reflect for a moment on their nature. A cloud is amorphous; when you look at one, you often see whatever your imagination suggests. A cloud looks impressive, but when you try to touch it you learn how insubstantial it really is. A cloud is, quite literally, nebulous. Above all, perhaps, a cloud is something that obscures your vision, that covers up the truth-revealing light of day. So clouds very aptly symbolize the mental obfuscation that prevails within the Thinking-Shop, captivating and bewitching Strepsiades.

After this elaborate choral entrance, Socrates resumes (365ff.), proclaiming that there is no Zeus in heaven: all the celestial weather phenomena that lead the vulgar to believe in him really have natural causes. He speaks of a heavenly vortex and Strepsiades misunderstands him, thinking that Vortex must be some new god who has replaced Zeus (380). For a goodly amount of time Socrates goes on revealing such physical mysteries and Strepsiades is deeply impressed. Then Socrates returns again to the subject of religion: the old man must learn to discount the old gods and swear by those worshipped within the Thinking-Shop, Chaos, the Clouds, and the almighty Tongue. An impressed Strepsiades pledges his loyalty to these novel deities.

After a conversation between Strepsiades and the chorus, Socrates asks him in more detail about his debt problem, but quickly gains the premonition that the fellow is too ignorant and backward to learn anything (490f.). Nonetheless, he takes him into the Thinking-Shop so that lessons in the fine art of bamboo-zling creditors can begin.

And so it goes. Strepsiades is initiated into further Thinking-Shop mysteries of the same hilariously weird sort, having to do with subtle verbal manipulations and logic-twisting, but it rapidly becomes apparent that the old man is simply too stupid to absorb this interesting stuff. Perceiving this, Socrates advises Strepsiades to send his son to school in his place (795). Pheidippides is promptly produced. Like any normal Athenian, he swears an oath by Zeus, and his father ridicules him for his old-fashioned notions. Hasn't the boy heard of the new god Vortex? Pheidippides thinks he is talking nonsense, that he has been driven crazy by those "bilious geniuses" Socrates and Chaerephon (830ff.). But, although harboring the deepest reservations about the lore of the Thinking-Shop and also about the merits of the project at hand, Pheidippides permits himself to be subjected to the new education. Thus far the boy, for all his enthusiasm for horses, is portrayed as a normal and healthy Athenian youth. The only reason why he permits himself to be enlisted in this enterprise seems to be a sense of filial duty. The contrast between this Pheidippides and the Pheidippides we meet later in the play is drawn with extreme sharpness.

Pheidippides' actual "education" (889ff.) consists of exposure to a debate between the Just Argument and the Unjust Argument. Since Socrates' claim is that he can make the worse argument appear the better and *vice versa*, what better than to present the two arguments onstage in personified form? Aristophanes has an occasional proclivity for translating abstractions into visual, reified terms. Thus, for instance, when the hero of *The Acharnians* procures a private peace for himself, this peace is both spoken of and shown to the audience in the concretized form of a skin full of finest wine. As we are also reminded by *The Wasps*'s dog-trial, much of Aristophanes' humor is as idiosyncratic visually as it is verbally, and we often cannot calculate the full comic effect of the plays if we do not imaginatively follow the action on the visual level while reading them.

As one would expect, the debate contrasts two styles of education. As one might not expect, to a remarkable degree it focuses on the single subject of sex. The Just Argument's premise—which proves to be the premise of the play as a whole—is first stated at 926ff.: that the kind of education supported by the Unjust Argument destroys young men, the underlying assumption being that education has the decisive power to mold character. More specifically, the Unjust Argument proclaims that his opponent will never get to teach Pheidippides: this argument is not just conducted in the abstract—they are competing for the boy's soul.

A certain amount is said about the Unjust Argument teaching him verbal trickery. When the two Arguments get down to business, they turn to sex. Like any good conservative, the Just Argument idealizes the past. Once upon a time justice and prudence flourished. Boys read the simple and manly poetry admired by their forefathers. If any lad were to develop an interest in trashy, newfangled stuff he received a beating (970ff.). But then he describes at length how the boys were obliged to act with moderation lest they become pederast-bait. The products of this education, combining exposure to poetry containing traditional values with enforced sexual repression, are model citizens who do not waste away their time with idle debate or courtroom wrangling. Thus were educated the stout souls who defeated the Persians at Marathon.

The Unjust Argument offers his rebuttal. He admits that he has received his name "because I was the first to figure out how to denounce established customs and laws" (1038f.): he is frankly in the business of overthrowing traditional values. He then subjects the Just Argument to a kind of cross-examination, and once again the subject is sex. Can the Just Argument name anybody who has ever profited from chastity? He supplies a couple of mythological examples, but the Unjust Argument shows precisely how flimsy they are. On the other hand (1072ff.) if you reckon up our essential pleasures (little boys and girls, doubtless to be employed as sexual toys, parties, eating, drinking, kissing) you will discover that life is not worth living without them. Nature itself compels you to sexual activity: such appeals to Nature's supreme imperatives are a stock item in the sophistic armory. If you commit adultery and are caught in the act, you are ruined. Or rather, you are ruined unless you are a good student of the Unjust Argument and know how to talk your way out of a jam. Then you will be free to indulge your real nature, regarding nothing as shameful (1078).

Look at Zeus himself—did he not do precisely the same? Here the Unjust Argument touches on a sensitive Greek nerve. How can religion be used to enjoin moral behavior when mythology and myth-based literature often represent them as behaving with immorality (as when Zeus seduces miscellaneous mortal girls, often to their sorrow)? As Greek civilization became increasingly sophisticated, the question of myth's presentation of the gods as amoral caused a good deal of discomfort to Greek thinkers and moralists. This is evidently why the poet Xenophanes of Colophon said that Homer and Hesiod, the first two poets to enshrine mythology in literature, deserved a good whipping. And, even though it is not the official reason Plato wanted to banish the mimetic arts from his ideal state, surely this problem was an important consideration.

So the upshot is that we are all wide-assed: that is to say, when an Athenian was caught in adultery, the standard punishment was to cram a radish up his rectum. Just consider: aren't lawyers recruited from the class of the wide-assed? The Just Argument is obliged to confess that they are. Well, what about the tragic poets? What about the orators? What, when you come right down to it, about the spectators right here in the theater? Admittedly they are wide-assed, and on that note the Just Argument is compelled to confess his defeat. He leaves the stage ripping off his clothes, begging Athens' buggers to accept him as one of their own.

Of course, on the level of sheer comedy, when the Unjust Argument extracts the concession that various categories of people, leading up to the present audience, are wide-assed, this is done in the interest of getting an escalating series of laughs. But something important is at stake. If you concede that all of us are just large and relatively hairless monkeys finding our deepest fulfillment in sexual shenanigans, then organized society and its conventions begin to look like nothing more than a monstrously hypocritical conspiracy of silence meant to camouflage our genuine natures. As the sophist Thrasymachus says in Book I of Plato's *Republic* (although he is talking about a quite different subject), once the superior man sees through such sham he is under no further obligation to take it seriously. Religion, high poetry, and other sources of traditional moral values can be dismissed as organs of this conspiracy, and the morality they enjoin can be disregarded. Thus a theoretical basis can be constructed for the injunction to regard nothing as shameful.

At length Socrates brings out Pheidippides, and Strepsiades is delighted with the result. Now his son is suitably pale and haggard: he looks like a good logic-chopper and his expression of injured innocence is "the regular Athenian face" (1175). Under catechism, Pheidippides displays his new prowess at debt-avoiding, by using against a creditor some verbal rigmarole based on the fact that the first day of the lunar month, when debts fall due, is called "the old and new day"—but how can a single debt be due on two separate days? A little extra display of linguistic expertise for show, and the creditor is sent packing. A second creditor appears but is likewise whipped off the stage when he cannot keep up with Pheidippides' verbal pyrotechnics.

At this point, Strepsiades and Pheidippides disappear from the stage as they chase away the pesky creditor, leaving the chorus alone to ruminate on developments (1303ff.). This would be the appropriate time for the chorus to congratulate Strepsiades on the success of his plan. But they know better. They predict that this success will rebound on Strepsiades: now that his boy has commenced a career of rascality, he himself will surely receive some evil from it. The time will come when he wishes that his son is a mute!

This prophecy is immediately fulfilled. As soon as the choral interlude ends, the father and son reappear; Strepsiades is crying "ow wow wow" since Pheidippides has just administered him a thrashing. The Athenians regarded a son's offering physical violence to his father with particular repugnance, as was reflected both in their writings and in their law code. Taking the intention for the deed, Athenian law regarded any such action as a form of parricide (cf. Strepsiades' use of this word at 1327). Nevertheless, when angrily challenged by Strepsiades, Pheidippides unrepentantly announces that he can defend his action with some further displays of Thinking-Shop logic.

But first Strepsiades explains to the audience how the beating occurred. When he first brought the boy home, he bid him sing an old song by Simonides. He refused disdainfully. So Strepsiades suggested something out of Aeschylus. Same answer. In response to a defeated concession that he could perform something modern, the boy launched into a passage by

Euripides describing incest between brother and sister. In horror, Strepsiades objected to this degenerate stuff, and Pheidippides gave him a thorough beating. Here is a humorous reversal of the situation described by the Just Argument in which boys who developed an interest in literary trash were spanked. Nevertheless the passage is curiously protracted beyond what is necessary to extract the obvious humor from this inversion, to the point that the reader may wonder about its dramatic relevance.

Then Pheidippides offers his defense. His essential talking point: when he was young, Strepsiades occasionally spanked him. Why? Because he loved his son. Well then, Strepsiades is now in his second childhood. Shouldn't a son reciprocate his love in the same manner? Strepsiades is thoroughly convinced by this rebuttal and is obliged to concede the propriety of his son's action. He is as hypnotized by the lore of the Thinking-Shop as ever. But then a remarkable reversal occurs, when Pheidippides goes on to the next point of his argument. By the same argument, he proposes that he must also give his mother a thumping (1443–6).

As soon as he hears these words Strepsiades undergoes a dramatic transformation. He immediately explodes in indignant rage, the scales drop from his eyes, and he admits his foolishness. He reasserts the reality of Zeus and the other traditional gods, and attacks the Thinking-Shop, burning it down with all its inmates. At the very end of the play he pronounces that they have paid the price for their blasphemy of the traditional gods (1509).

This transformation is very remarkable, both for its abruptness and for its violence. What precisely has happened to disabuse Strepsiades of his illusions and to trigger his murderous attack? It looks as if *The Clouds* builds to a single grand climax, more than does any other Aristophanic comedy, and this climax is set off by Pheidippides' announcement of his plans for his mother. We must ask why.

Pheidippides' threat to "thump his mother" looks dangerously equivocal. The reason most scholars have not appreciated this is that evidently the verb Pheidippides uses, *typto*, is not otherwise employed in extant classical Greek with a sexual connotation.[8] But this objection is probably not fatal, since verbs for striking and hitting are frequently used as slang synonyms for sexual intercourse in Greek and in many other languages. And in any event, the meaning of the expression could easily be made clear if the actor playing Pheidippides were to deliver these lines suggestively or make a suitably improper gesture (notice how the verb is repeated within a very few lines, as if Aristophanes is laying particular stress on its sinister implications).

The advantage of thinking that Pheidippides is issuing a not-very-veiled threat to reenact the Oedipal situation by violence is that it explains several things that would otherwise remain puzzling. In the first place, if Pheidippides in the Thinking-Shop was exposed to the new kind of education espoused by the Unjust Argument, it would make excellent dramatic sense to represent him as becoming depraved specifically in the area that the Unjust Argument has been talking about. Pheidippides has heard, understood, and internalized the message that nothing is shameful. Now he plans on translating this doctrine into action.

Pheidippides' new enthusiasm for Euripides can now be seen to be the first warning sign that all is not well with him. Of course, a subsidiary purpose of this passage is to get in a comic sideswipe against the poet. In *The Frogs* Aristophanes will return to the accusation that Euripidean tragedies are full of sex-crazed women, incest, and similar erotic trash. But the fundamental point is that his enthusiasm for Euripides and his specific fascination with incest are symptoms of depravity and signs of things to come.

The interpretation that Pheidippides is threatening to rape his mother and reenact the Oedipal situation is useful because it ties the debate between the Arguments more firmly into the fabric of the overall plot and reveals the relevance of the squabble over Aeschylus and Euripides. But its chief value is that it supplies a full and adequate explanation of Strepsiades' abrupt change of attitude and thus explicates the play's climax. For if Strepsiades can be convinced by twisted logic to accept his own beating with equanimity, it is not self-evident why he should regard the prospect of his wife receiving a similar beating with such outrage.

Some critics claim that *The Clouds* is the only Aristophanic play that does not have a happy ending. This appraisal is not quite right. The play ends with a strong note of justice being done, ever an affirmative conclusion. Poetic justice is executed on Strepsiades. The ultimate joke of the play is, as suggested earlier in this chapter, that he gets more than he bargains for, so that his bright idea explodes in his face. He wanted to transform his son into a pettifogger, but he gets back from the Thinking-Shop a monster and, with impeccable logic, becomes the monster's first victim.

The ending is also affirmative because, besides overthrowing the Thinking-Shop, Strepsiades scores the victory of regaining contact with his roots. By moving to the city and marrying an aristocrat, and then by becoming involved with the Thinking-Shop and its works, he has increasingly been hornswoggled and intimidated by the denizens of the city and lost touch with his peasant origins. Now, at the last, he discovers that his traditional values—above all his loyalty to the Olympian gods—are fully vindicated, as is his preference for the good old-time art of Simonides and Aeschylus. So the hell with the great god Vortex and all such nonsense! Surely this triumph of values and outlooks that Aristophanes supports throughout his works counts as a truly happy ending.

Something else can be added about this happy ending. If *The Wasps* and *The Clouds* are linked by exploring father–son relationships, they are also linked by a second common denominator. They both deal with the city-country dichotomy. Philocleon and Strepsiades are both recruited from the same class of healthy, down-to-earth peasants that furnishes other Aristophanic heroes (such as Dicaeopolis in *The Acharnians* and Trygaeus in *Peace*). These heroes have much in common: loyalty to traditional values, and earthy directness coupled with a disdain for pomposity, pretense, and fraud (and also, with the exception of Strepsiades until the very end, a keen eye for penetrating the same). Each of these plays, in its own way, deals with a situation in which a peasant-hero turns the tables on city slickers who threaten to take advantage of him in some way, swindle him, or convert him into an effete or otherwise distorted city man like themselves. For some reason, stereotypes involving denizens of the city and those of the country are perennially common in Western comedy. In the present case, the denizens of the Thinking-Shop are preeminently urban creatures, and when looked at from this angle Socrates is nothing but a particular brand of city slicker. By very different routes Philocleon and Strepsiades arrive at what is remarkably the same place: at the ends of their respective plays, they both reaffirm their essential peasant natures and the virtues Aristophanes thought were located most firmly in the Attic countryside.

This is a thought worth keeping, for the city-country dichotomy will reappear in later classical comedy, again associated with questions about the relation of sons to their fathers. Then it will appear in transmuted guises with very different values attached to the two sides. But nonetheless here is another thematic thread running through the history of ancient comedy and beyond.

Before taking leave of Aristophanes, we should take a brief glance at another of his works. At *Clouds* 527 the chorus refers to a previous play with the allusive phrase "the chaste man and the bugger." They are speaking about *The Banqueteers*, Aristophanes' first play, produced in 427 B.C. This play has not been preserved, but some tantalizing information about it can be recovered from quotations preserved by later writers.

The premise was that a father has two sons, one of whom receives a traditional education and turns out a modest and respectable young man. The other receives a modern sophistic education and is morally corrupted and also, as some fragments indicate, an alcoholic fop with a head crammed with uselessly recondite book learning. Even worse, he is also made into an artful courtroom wrangler.

Unfortunately the plot is not known. In one fragment an unidentified speaker threatens to bring suit against someone for falsely claiming to be an Athenian citizen. The depraved son may have brought this suit against his father. The point cannot be proven, but since other fragments pertain to the courtroom it is quite possible that the play contained a trial scene. Certainly, it would fit in well with *The Banqueteers*'s theme to have one son remain properly filial and the other turn against his father.

This play must have resembled *The Clouds* at the thematic level. Both dealt with the idea that education determines character and contrasted the soundly old-fashioned with the dangerously newfangled. *The Banqueteers* also contains a son who carries the quest for freedom and fun too far, and it may have explored a father–son conflict. We know nothing about the father in the play, save that he was presumably portrayed as a sensible conservative. We do not know if the son's modern education was the father's idea or, if so, what his reasons may have been for having his boy brought up in this way. Was he too represented as a countryman, so that again the son's depravity was represented as an example of the corruptive force of city life?

Chapter 2

Menander and the Greek New Comedy

The New Comedy

After the fifth century B.C. the nature of Greek comedy began to change rapidly. Signs of change are visible even in Aristophanes' last two surviving plays, *The Ecclesiazusae* and *Plutus*. Known as New Comedy, the kind of comedy that finally emerged from a half century of evolutionary developments and false starts was radically different in its nature.

In accordance with the program of this study, in looking at Aristophanic comedy, we have been primarily concerned with his comic handling of father-son situations. But no attempt has been made to conceal the fact that this is only one element in Aristophanes' much more complex comic view of life, and that his primary concern was the wider world of the Athenian *polis*. *The Wasps* and *The Clouds* are about father–son relationships, but they are multivalent plays that are about much else too: high matters dealing with corrupted democracy, bad law, and corrupting newfangled education, with numerous comic sideswipes taken at a host of other targets. As we have seen, Aristophanes' favorite technique for dealing with such serious issues was to handle them fantastically. But if the Old Comedy had been a comic form that, paradoxically, dealt with the immediacy of the Athenian city-state through bold excursions into fantasy, the New Comedy was firmly centered in the realities of bourgeois domestic life, or more precisely a rather idealized and stylized version thereof. This new kind of comedy was concerned with crises and contentions within the middle-class *oikos* (the extended family, including retainers and slaves) and the problems of young lovers trying to overcome obstacles in order to be united.

New Comedy was also snob comedy. A snob may be defined as an amateur sociologist who likes to categorize people according to their social classes and who diligently observes the nuances of behavior that betray class background. New Comedy characters tend to be readily identifiable representatives of distinct social classes and a lot of attention is paid to their interaction both with their peers and with representatives of other classes. Of course the danger inherent in snobbism is a tendency to think in stereotyped terms, and New Comedy is scarcely innocent of this shortcoming.

The essential reason for this shift in focus can be located in the radically changed nature of Athenian society. Between the time of the heyday of Old Comedy and that when New Comedy flourished, much had happened to Athens: her resounding defeat in the Peloponnesian war; internal upheavals when democracy was temporarily overthrown; further military and economic reversals over the first half of the next century. The net result of this series of catastrophes is that individual Athenians were driven in upon themselves. Although in the fifth century B.C. Athenians of course had family lives, they had also been passionately interested and involved in the public affairs of their city-state, and Aristophanic comedy dealt with Athenians both in their public and private capacities. As wider public outlets for their energies and enthusiasms became decreasingly available, private concerns and hedonism seem to have loomed all the larger for many Athenians. Therefore the revolution in fictive comedy reflected a revolution in real life.

For there is plenty of evidence that in the fourth century B.C. most Athenians centered their interest on their private affairs, and that to a large extent this reorientation took the form of pleasure-seeking. If stock characters such as courtesans, parasites, and professional chefs make their debut as comic characters, this is only because their real-life equivalents were achieving something like "superstar" status. Likewise, New Comedy knows of something that seems more or less to approximate the modern experience of romantic love, and this is a preoccupation that we hear little or nothing about in the fifth century B.C.[1] Certainly it plays no part in the plays of Aristophanes.

Between the Old and the New Comedy existed a form that flourished during the first half of the fourth century B.C., called the Middle Comedy. We only possess fragments of lost Middle Comedy plays, and the curious thing about them is that the large majority dwell obsessively and extravagantly on the single subject of food in general and gourmet cooking in particular. There is something repulsive and pathological about this monomania. Possibly it is a reaction to the fact that after the turn of the century Athens was repeatedly visited, for the first time in its history, by famine. In any event, this was obviously a form of comedy leading to a dead end and it is hard to feel much regret over the fact that no Middle Comedy survives.

Such, in short, was the Athenian society of the fourth century B.C., which was first mesmerized, and then conquered by Macedonia. Perceiving the growing threat from the north, Demosthenes tried to arouse the Athenians and recall them to something like the public-spiritedness of the previous century. But he got nowhere, because the inertia of their newfound selfishness and hedonism proved too great to budge. New Comedy is a characteristic product of this society, and addresses its tastes and concerns. And of course, once the Athenians were defeated by the Macedonians and lost their independence, being governed by a series of foreign generalissimos, a kind of comedy concerned exclusively with domestic matters proved to be politically safe and noncontroversial.

Old Comedy frequently made fun of actual individuals and, as in the case of Socrates in *The Clouds*, could even make them stage characters. Even its fictional characters are rugged and often memorable individuals. New Comedy, on the other hand, typically dealt with a stock set of characters: the adolescent boy in love, the grouchy old man, the amiable old man, the clever rascal-slave, the parasite, etc. This reliance on stock characters was carried to such a point that any theater company playing New Comedy would use the same set of standard masks representing each of these character types, immediately identifiable to the audience for what they were.[2] Even the names by which these individuals are called are remarkably stereotyped (such as old men named Demeas or star-crossed lovers named Moschion).

New Comedy was written for a changed, more polite society, and for a society that was far less willing to concede playwrights unlimited freedom of speech. Therefore two of the most striking characteristics of Aristophanic comedy are all but entirely missing: obscenity and humor insulting to actual Athenians. (This raises an interesting question for which I cannot supply an answer: what is the relation of this intensified enthusiasm for private hedonism and new standards of public decorum?)

We have already seen that, after the deaths of Euripides and Sophocles, Attic tragedy became as fossilized as Aristophanes predicted it would be in *The Frogs*. While tragedies continued to be written, only comedy remained one of the lively arts. Accordingly, some of the features that had characterized tragedy in the days of its greatness now devolved upon comedy.

The first such feature was a new interest in the construction of comic plots. Although parts of Aristophanes' plays are carefully structured (for example, the *parabasis*, the part of the play where the chorus addresses the audience, and the *agon*, or formal debate, were written according to strict structural formulae), they are often rather episodic and most are not constructed so as to build inexorably toward a single plot reversal, a single comic climax. In the New Comedy, on the other hand, the plot is very much the thing. We do not possess the second Book of Aristotle's *Poetics*, in which comedy was treated—some scholars question whether such a document ever existed—but if we could read it, doubtless we would discover that a large portion was devoted to making a parallel point to that made about tragedy: that comedy's effect is best produced by a well-crafted plot.[3] Aristotle would have argued that the comic climax is secured by the same devices as the tragic one: *anagnoresis*, or revelation, and *peripeteia*, or climactic plot reversal. He may also have had a theory that such plot devices produced a comic equivalent of tragedy's catharsis.[4] If the *Poetics* did contain these elements, it very much reflected the tastes of the age, and if Aristotle was read by contemporary playwrights his pronouncements may well have reinforced their emphasis on plot construction. According to a famous anecdote, Menander once explained that he had just completed a play—now all he had to do was write its dialogue. This story demonstrates the tremendous importance placed on plotting.

Perhaps because of the all-importance of plot construction, the role of the chorus diminished almost to the vanishing point. With the exception of his last two plays, Aristophanes wrote choral drama, as is betokened by the number of his comedies that take their titles from the chorus's identity. In the fourth century B.C. playwrights ceased to write choral passages and merely inserted the word CHORUS in their scripts to indicate, essentially, act-divisions. Probably they were indifferent to the contents of such choral passages precisely because they regarded choruses as intrusive elements that did not foster the advancement of tightly constructed dramatic structures. (The diminished role of choruses may also have been introduced as an economy measure.)

From what has just been said it should be obvious that New Comedy's indebtedness to its comic predecessor was not great. Its indebtedness to Greek tragedy is considerably more visible. Most particularly, many New Comedies (and their Roman counterparts) contain important elements derived from such Euripidean plays of intrigue and romance as *Ion*, *Iphigeneia in Tauris*, and *Helen*, since they frequently turn on situations of mistaken identities or misunderstood motives, where the revelation of the true identity or motive produces a recognition scene that elicits the plot's climax. Other familiar features of later comedy that are derived from tragedy are evidenced in the play we are about to consider, Menander's *Dyscolus*: the use of expository prologues spoken by a deity, and the idea that the unfolding of a plot is really the result of the god's secret manipulations.

With its stock characters, stereotyped situations, and relentless interest in middle-class domestic life, the New Comedy inevitably invites comparison with one of the standard entertainment genres of our times, television situation comedy. And the comparison proves to be quite instructive. In the early days of situation comedy, critical viewers were prone to write the genre off as a mindless and predictable form of entertainment existing in a sort of Never-Never Land of idealized bourgeois life ("chewing gum for the eyes").[5] As the form developed we have learned that this appraisal is not necessarily true, that situation comedy can be converted into a vehicle for serious social commentary and probing psychological analysis. Although some critics have been willing to adopt an equally dismissive attitude toward New and Roman Comedy, we should be prepared for the possibility that this view is likewise mistaken.

Menander and *Dyscolus*

As with the Old Comedy, there were a number of practitioners of the New Comedy. But just as the Old Comedy was so dominated by Aristophanes that his work has virtually become synonymous with the form, so too there was a single outstanding writer of the New Comedy, Menander (ca. 342–291 B.C.).

Until the present century, Menander and his contemporaries were known to us principally by reputation and because a number of their plays were subsequently adapted by the Roman playwrights Plautus and Terence. But thanks to a number of remarkable papyrological discoveries, we now possess one of Menander's plays, *Dyscolus* (The grouch) of 317 B.C., in virtually complete form. Considerable portions of several others are preserved.

One of these, *Samia* (The girl from Samos), deals with a father-son relationship. Less than half of the play is preserved, so that it is not worth examining it in detail here, but the play's father-son tension may be noted in passing. The Athenian gentleman Demeas has an adopted son Moschion, and he unfairly suspects the boy of having had an affair with his Samian mistress, leading to the birth of an illegitimate child. In a soliloquy at the beginning of Act V, Moschion vents his indignation at being wrongly suspected of such a misdeed. He is too dutiful a son to run away from home, but there can be no harm in shaking up the old man by pretending that he will do so.

So this is one of those plays that turns on a misunderstanding and on misinterpreted motives, and doubtless in the play's conclusion (which is not preserved) these misunderstandings are cleared up. This father and son are not really rivals for the affections of one woman (or, perhaps one should more bluntly say, competing for control of a single sexual object). But Menander at least manages to raise the specter of such a father-son rivalry. In other comedies such a competition, richly endowed with Oedipal overtones, does actually exist.

Other lost plays by Menander dealt with father-son relationships, such as *Dis Exapaton* (The double deceiver), the Greek model for Plautus' *Bacchides*, and *Adelphoi* (The brothers), the prototype of Terence's *Adelphoe*. Both of these works will be touched on below.

Dyscolus does not have to do with a father-son relationship, but it deals with generational conflict in a more generalized way and resonates with some of the other plays considered here. The play's central character, Cnemon, is portrayed as an embittered misanthrope, attempting without much success to work an isolated farm in the outback of Attica. Because of his misanthropy, his wife has left him, taking with her a young son by a previous marriage, Gorgias. Mother and son now occupy the farm next door to Cnemon's. In the prologue Pan, who has a shrine adjacent to Cnemon's farm, sets the stage, sketches the background, and prepares the audience for the following action. It seems that Cnemon has a daughter who, unlike her father, has pleased the god by her constant piety. The god therefore intends to reward her. Pan has cast a spell on a decent young city fellow who has been vacationing in these parts, Sostratus, so that he has fallen violently in love with the girl. In fact, here he comes now.

The god retires and the love-smitten Sostratus enters, accompanied by a lightly ironic friend, Chaireas, whom he has asked to help him in his suit. They try, but it is no go: Cnemon violently rebuffs any attempt at communication. By the end of Act I, the plight of Cnemon's daughter is clear. She is marooned on this isolated farm. With a father like Cnemon, her prospects are bleak, and love is entirely thwarted. In Act II, Gorgias, Cnemon's erstwhile stepson, befriends Sostratus. He offers some advice: Cnemon will certainly reject his suit if he thinks he is a soft city liver. But if he sees him out in the fields, Cnemon might adopt a more favorable attitude. So Sostratus resolves to try his hand at farming.

When they go off a couple of servants in Gorgias' household come on. They are preparing a sacrifice because Gorgias' mother has had a most alarming dream. She has dreamt that Pan has placed Sostratus in chains and was forcing him to work the soil with a mattock. Naturally the dream is one of those significant ones: the chains are really those of love, and the purpose of this passage is to remind the audience that everything occurring in the play results from Pan's behind-the-scenes machinations.

In Act III the people who are going to make the offering to Pan begin to assemble and, as the onlooking Cnemon sarcastically observes, this religious rite bears more than a slight resemblance to a picnic. Sostratus joins the merrymakers: he has a full set of sore muscles, and has learned much about the hard effort involved in working a farm. But at the end of the act a crisis begins to develop. Simiche, Cnemon's single servant, appears in distress. She has dropped a bucket down his well. Trying to rescue the bucket, she used a mattock attached to a rope, but the rope broke and so the mattock is also lost now. One of Gorgias' servants offers to help but is rudely rebuffed by Cnemon. Then the sacrifice intervenes and the act ends. But by the beginning of the next act, the crisis has greatly worsened. Cnemon tried to retrieve the bucket and the mattock, but slipped and fell down, so now he too is in the well. Gorgias and Sostratus are obliged to rescue him, with Gorgias doing most of the work while Sostratus moons at his daughter.

Cnemon is so impressed by his rescue that he gratefully informs Gorgias that he is now his heir. He gives him half his property to support his ex-wife and daughter and entrusts him with finding the daughter a suitable husband. Sostratus is promptly produced to fill this role. Sostratus' father Callipides makes a brief appearance and the act draws to a close.

The fifth act begins with an interview between Sostratus and Callipides. Sostratus has had a bright idea: why not turn it into a double wedding by marrying Gorgias to his own sister? At first Callipides objects on the grounds that he does not want two impoverished young men in the family, but since he is portrayed as a preeminently affable and tolerant man, his objections are quickly worn down. In fact, he proves to be very well-to-do.

Besides settling a handsome dowry on his own daughter, he waives Gorgias' rather overgenerous offer of a dowry for his sister since he knows Gorgias is poor.

But even if the play's romantic problems have been resolved, some important business remains to be settled. Being rescued from the well, to be sure, has constituted an important turning-point for Cnemon. His attitude has been changed to the extent he was willing to acknowledge Gorgias' true worth and bring himself to part both with his property and his daughter. But he can scarcely be said to be fully rehabilitated. The problem of his isolation remains outstanding. The resolution of this issue is treated in a rather symbolic way. There is to be a wedding celebration, and although Cnemon has even permitted his servant Simiche to join in, he himself is reluctant to attend. So he has not fully abandoned his hermit-hood. The problem is handled by Gorgias' household servants, who describe to him the party revelry and in the end more or less compel him to go along and join in the drinking, singing, and dancing. Thus, we are given to understand, his reintegration into society will begin.

In the course of *Dyscolus* the reader is furnished with remarkably particularized information about Cnemon's farm. It is situated in an isolated locale in Phyle, a mountainous deme on Mount Parnes on Attica's Boeotian border. It is therefore, as one would imagine, a rocky and difficult terrain. At the beginning of the play Pan summarizes the situation of somebody working a farm in such a landscape with the words "Phylaeans are able to farm this stony ground." At 603ff. Cnemon's hardscrabble existence is described in more detail: "Poor man, what a life he leads. That's your genuine Attic farmer. He struggles with stony soil that grows thyme and sage, getting a good deal of pain and no profit." The validity of this assessment is shown graphically when the townsman Sostratus tries his hand at working the soil with a mattock and quickly discovers what a difficult task it is for the inexperienced (522ff.).

In view of this generally bleak picture, therefore, it is surprising to be informed (327) that Cnemon's farm is worth two talents. On the basis of a remark in an approximately contemporary speech wrongly attributed to Demosthenes, we happen to know that at this time it was difficult but not impossible to live on a farm costing three-quarters of a talent. In his note on line 327

E. W. Handley, author of an excellent annotated edition of *Dyscolus*, supplies the obvious answer for this seeming factual contradiction. "Allowing, as seems necessary, that values in Comedy may be conventionally higher than real values, the estate is still a considerable one, large enough to make it remarkable, indeed absurd, that Knemon works it alone."[6] Precisely. Cnemon's unenviable position is of his own making. If he were not antisocial and if he had helpers, one feels, the farm could be made to produce crops commensurate with the potential implied by its cash value. So even before falling in the well he pays a heavy and visible price for his social alienation. Even more, it does not seem far-fetched to see this isolated, stony, and all but barren hilltop farm as the outward sign and symbol of Cnemon's equally desolate spiritual condition.

On the tragic stage, when a character has a severely misguided attitude, there is usually a religious dimension to his wrongheadedness. The title character in Sophocles' *Ajax*, for example, rashly boasts that he needs no help from the gods, and his bullheaded Creon is dead sure, much evidence notwithstanding, that his desires and those of the gods are exactly congruent. So too, evidently, part of Cnemon's problem is religious. At the beginning of the play Pan, to whom the shrine next door to Cnemon's farm is dedicated, says, "He's never volunteered a polite greeting to anyone except myself . . . and that's only because he lives beside me and can't help passing my door. And I'm quite sure that, as soon as he does, he promptly regrets it." This is further evidence of Cnemon's curmudgeonly nature, but the contrast with the conspicuous piety of Cnemon's daughter also described by Pan is notable and suggests that Cnemon has done more than just sever his ties with humankind. He has turned his back on the larger and more comprehensive society of men and the gods.

In fact, there is something very tragedy-like about the entire play. From both the prologue and the dream-description, the audience is given to understand that Pan has set in motion a scheme for rewarding the piety of Cnemon's daughter. Although the characters involved in the story are blissfully unaware of his agency, and think they are merely being tossed about by the vagaries of Tyche (Fortune personified as a divinity), the audience knows better. On the basis of this prologue, in which the god shares his secrets with the audience, what seem to the characters to be a string of coincidences and accidents—above all the string of coincidental mishaps that ultimately puts Cnemon down in the well, which just happen to occur during a community act of piety toward Pan—are understood by us to be the results of the god's behind-the-scenes wire-pulling. This sets up the possibility of a comic equivalent of tragic irony. And the idea of using a god's introductory monologue to let the audience in on the secret that the ensuing dramatic action is actually the result of that god's invisible manipulations distinctly reminds one of the use of the same dramatic technique in such tragedies as Euripides' *Hippolytus.*

Menander presents us with something not found in previous comedy, the picture of a man's transformation. Here we have as dourly agelastic an old man as we could hope to find. Because of his condition he stands in the way of the fulfillment of young love, an obstacle to his daughter's marriage. In the more combative world of Old Comedy he would have been portrayed entirely without sympathy, would have had to be sent down to defeat and humiliation. But Menander's world is gentler and his plays are more psychologically insightful. (This might seem a bit paradoxical, since he employs stock characters, but one might again compare the way latter-day situation comedies can be employed to explore human character, although they still feature stereotypes.) Therefore Menander raises a new possibility. Rather than being a "villain" who has to be overcome by a pugnacious comic hero, Cnemon is a spiritually misguided man in need of reform. The god to whom he is disrespectful, who would be fully entitled to wreak vengeance, creates the conditions that bring about his saving transformation. Ostensibly he does so to bring about the marriage of Sostratus and Cnemon's daughter, which results from the string of events that begins when the bucket falls down the well. But who is to say that Cnemon's change of heart has not been a second goal of the god all along? If ancient comedy knows of two types of old men, fun-loving and agelastic (the old man who is in touch with Dionysus and the old man who is not), Menander raises the possibility that the one kind can be changed into the other. When Cnemon emerges from the well a changed man, he has undergone an almost spiritual death and rebirth.

Another point worth making involves the contrast between Cnemon and Callipides. On the stage, if you want to emphasize one character's salient traits, a good way to drive this home is to bring on a character with the opposite ones. Thus, if you want to highlight Antigone's determination, you give her a scene with compliant Ismene. If there are two kinds of comic fathers, agelastic and tolerant, fun-hating and fun-loving, forbiddingly authoritarian and genially tolerant, what better way to highlight the contrast than to bring them on stage. To be sure, in *Dyscolus* Callipides' character is not deeply explored and he and Cnemon do not have any interaction. But this onstage contrast of father-types points the way to a dramatic technique in which the differences between them are more fully investigated and in which they are directly confronted with each other. In some of the Roman comedies we shall be considering, this technique is put into play.

Matters would be simple, simple to the point of fatuity and tedium, if Cnemon's transformation consisted simply of learning the lessons that "no man is an island," that "people need people." But something else is at stake. We have a highly interesting interpretation of *Dyscolus* from later antiquity. In his *Rustic Letters* Aelian, a Greek writer of the Roman Imperial period whose life spanned the second and third centuries A.D., includes several fictitious letters exchanged between Cnemon and Callippides (as Aelian prefers to spell his name). One pair is especially germane (xv, xvi). They have been summarized by a recent writer:

> The second dyad of letters...between Kallippides and Knemon is on the subject of an offering to Pan. Kallippides' letter sarcastically proposes that Knemon attend a feast and sacrifice for Pan which the former is planning. Knemon, in his letter, brusquely rejects the offer. Aelian satirizes them both, but more importantly captures Menander's criticism of the essential qualities of impious behavior: (1) religious observance motivated by something other than devotion and love for the god himself; and (2) a self-absorption so deep that even one's gods reflect one's personality.
>
> Kallippides begins his letter by stating that Knemon, as a wild and solitary individual, is a wickedly impious man. So to assuage his *dyskoleia* Knemon should participate in the feast by drinking heavily, singing to a flute girl's tunes and perhaps waylaying an errant maid-

en. Knemon responds with characteristic vitriol to Kallippides' insincere attempt to socialize him. Crowds, wine, song and potential trysts do not appeal to him; he finds them repulsive. As for Pan and the other gods, he salutes them as he passes their shrines, but he does not sacrifice to them. Why not? He does not want to bother them.[7]

It may seem rather remarkable that Aelian fixes on impiety as Cnemon's salient trait, for his manifold other bad characteristics are at first sight more conspicuous. After all, one can find plenty wrong with misanthropy without having to bring religious considerations into the picture. But Aelian's diagnosis has much to recommend it. To understand it, we must pause a moment and consider exactly what kind of god Pan is.

Whatever its date may be, one of the most important ancient literary texts about this god is the *Homeric Hymn to Pan* (XIX). The poet begins:

> Muse, tell me about Pan, the dear son of Hermes, with his goat's feet and two horns—a lover of merry noise. Through wooded glades he wanders with dancing nymphs who foot it upon some sheer cliff's edge, calling upon Pan, the shepherd-god, long-haired, unkempt.[8]

The Hymn goes on to relate the circumstances of his birth, and concludes by stating how when he was born "...all the immortals were glad in heart and Bacchic Dionysus especially." It more than hints at the fact that Pan is a god with very strong Dionysiac associations. Like Dionysus, Pan roams the wild places, accompanied by his rout of nymphs. With his goat's head and feet he is extremely satyrlike, and indeed Dionysus' attendant satyrs are sometimes called *panes*.

In this play Pan acts as a kind of rustic surrogate for Dionysus. Aelian, at any rate, seems to think so, for when Callipides tries to convert Cnemon into a social animal he does so by urging him to behave precisely in the manner of a celebrant of a Dionysiac festive holiday. This is of course suggested by *Dyscolus's* conclusion, in which the wedding party is co-opted as a symbol of socialization generally. Just as with other agelastic old men in ancient comedy, the religious aspect of Cnemon's spiritual bleakness lies in the fact that he is out of touch with Dionysus.

If this diagnosis is correct, then an ending that would merely make Cnemon adopt a "no man is an island" philosophy, relent his misanthropy, and permit his daughter to marry, would be an incomplete and not entirely satisfying conclusion. The genuine transformation of his personality must have a religious dimension. And indeed it does. In the play's concluding scene the servants compel a more or less reluctant Cnemon to join in the wedding party. They describe the dancing to him and inform him that he will be expected to join in the dance. Cnemon may not find this a particularly appetizing prospect, but he does allow himself to be led off to the party.

This image of a dancing old man evokes time-honored and powerful associations. *The Wasps* ends with Philocleon reasserting his inner youthful vigor by outdancing his rivals, and one thinks once more of those two decrepit old men, King Cadmus and Teiresias the seer, going out into the countryside to join in the dancing in Euripides' *The Bacchae*. Cnemon, like it or not, is going to become another dancing old man, dancing in honor of Dionysus. From this Dionysiac viewpoint, which is the innate view of comedy and of comedy's festival, going to the party and joining in the dance is a necessary part of his rehabilitation.

Dyscolus is not a father-son comedy, but it still deals with the conflict of generations. On the one hand we have the world of the old and maladjusted fun-hater (although, admittedly, a remarkably small world, having a population of one old man, one serving woman, and a forlorn daughter). On the other, we have the world of the other characters of the play, who are all fun-loving, properly socialized, and characterized as thoroughly attractive youths (or, in the case of Callipides, young at heart). The play deals with the collision of these two worlds and the victory of the latter over the former, with an attendant triumph of one set of values over the another. So, if you care to look at it in this way, *Dyscolus* also presents a conflict between generations with, as usual, the fulfillment of young love at stake.

A final point about *Dyscolus*. We have seen that on the Aristophanic stage the struggle between the fun-loving hero and his antagonists is coordinated with another form of contention, that between city and country. For some reason (which scholarship has not fully explored), Aristophanic heroes tend to be peasants and the healthy values they represent are shown to be best located in the countryside. The antagonists they must overcome are denizens of the city. City-country tensions are also visible in

Dyscolus, but with the polarities reversed: here the country-side stands for unhealthy and unnatural isolation and part of Cnemon's dour misanthropy seems to have to do with his peasantlike nature. His stepson Gorgias is portrayed as a farmer but nonetheless as comparatively polished and urbane, and Sostratus, Callipides, and Chaireas are city men, all presented in a thoroughly favorable light. In the Roman plays we are about to examine, the same city–country tensions reappear, with a conservative and austere life-style located in the country and a more liberal and hedonistic one in the city. Since comedy favors hedonism, city life is routinely portrayed as vastly preferable to life down on the farm.

There is an interesting parallel between Cnemon's situation and that of Dicaeopolis, the peasant-hero of Aristophanes' *The Acharnians.* Disgusted with the Peloponnesian War, Dicaeopolis abandons Athens and returns to the deserted countryside, where he and his family live in magnificent isolation. Aristophanes portrays this as a moral victory. This contrast suggests that Aristophanes and Menander had very different attitudes toward such subjects as individualism and socialization.

Chapter 3

Plautus and the Nature of Roman Comedy

Plautine Comedy

Roman literature began as a literature of translation and adaptation of Greek originals in the genres of epic, tragedy, and comedy. Roman comedies were, with the sole known exception of Plautus' *Amphitryo*, based on New Comedy models. Although there were a number of Roman comic poets, all that remains consists of the corpus of plays by Titus Maccius Plautus (ca. 254–184 B.C.) and Publius Terentius Afer, better known simply as Terence (ca. 195–159 B.C.). Unlike Greek comedy, Roman comedies were not performed in the specific setting of festivals sacred to Dionysus. They were produced in connection with various religious holidays, on temporary stages erected in the Forum. Politicians wanting to burnish their public images subsidized the performances, so that the whole populace was able to watch these plays for free. Roman comedies were therefore a kind of festive comedy no less than their Greek equivalents.

In the course of his great *History of Rome* the nineteenth-century historian Theodor Mommsen unburdened himself of what must be one of the most comprehensive blasts ever leveled against a literary genre.[1] The whole thing is far too long to reproduce here, but a couple of high points may be quoted. Of Greek New Comedy he opined (in a work written before any significant New Comedy papyri had been discovered):

> No special accusation may be brought from a historico-moral point of view against poets in general, nor ought it to be made matter of individual reproach to the particular poet that he occupies the level of his epoch: comedy was not the cause but the effect of the corruption that prevailed in the national life. But it is necessary, more especially with a view to estimate correctly the influence of these comedies on the life of the Roman people, to point out the abyss which yawned beneath all that polish and elegance. The coarsenesses and obscenities which Menander indeed in some measure avoided . . . are the least part of the evil. Features far worse are the dreadful aspect of life as a desert in which the only oases are lovemaking and intoxication, [and] the fearfully prosaic monotony.[2]

Turning to Roman comedy, he wrote:

> If therefore the literary historian, while fully acknowledging the very respectable talents of the Roman comedians, cannot recognize in their mere stock of translations a product either artistically important or artistically pure, the judgment of history respecting its moral aspects must necessarily be far more severe. The Greek comedy which formed its basis was morally of little consequence, inasmuch as it was simply on the same level of corruption with its audience; but the Roman drama was, at this epoch when men were wavering between the old austerity and the new corruption, the great school at once of Hellenism and of vice. This Attico-Roman comedy, with its prostitution of body and soul usurping the name of love—equally immoral in shamelessness and in sentimentality—with its offensive and unnatural magnanimity, with its uniform glorification of a life of debauchery, with its mixture of rustic coarseness and foreign refinement, was one continuous lesson of Romano-Hellenic demoralization, and was felt as such.[3]

Even if the moral judgment of a nineteenth-century German is set aside, Mommsen's bill of particulars remains impressive. Of course this extremely hostile appraisal would not be worth quoting here if he had not managed to articulate a number of attitudes that many other readers have more or less shared. Such a reaction to Roman comedy is, one feels, dreadfully wrong, and it is important to show why.

The source of this view is readily identified. Most classicists have an understanding of the rise of Greek New Comedy that is ultimately indebted to what later Greeks themselves (notably the literary historian "Platonius" and the Byzantine scholar John Tzetzes) wrote on the subject. According to this historical model, the decline of the Old Comedy was associated with changing political conditions, under which the kind of freedom of speech necessary for Aristophanes' political commentary was no longer available. Therefore Old Comedy was replaced by a kind of comedy devoid of any serious political, social, or intellectual content. It was satisfactorily innocuous and hence could be performed in any number of social and political settings without risk of giving offense. Both because of its uncontroversial nature and because of the universality of domestic life and the immediate recognizability of the situations that tend to develop in the bosom of the family, the New Comedy was admirably suited for exportation to Rome.

Given this set of assumptions, it is easy to see why many readers have found it easy to develop an impression (although not necessarily as disdainful a one as Mommsen's) that both the New Comedy and its Roman descendants have, in effect, marginalized comedy by making it a rather insipid form of popular entertainment, and have in their minds compared it unfavorably with the content-rich comedy of Aristophanes.

But every play is a social construction, and this must be a difficult task—more likely an impossible one—to write one without consciously or unconsciously introducing any social or political content whatsoever. It is both striking and dismaying that some of the attitudes expressed in the preceding paragraph are visible in the writings of Plautus' warmest supporters and most penetrating analysts no less than in those of his severest detractors. Despite the very disparate attitudes displayed in their work, traces of such assumptions are visible in, say, Erich Segal's highly influential study of Plautus, no less than in his detractors (Segal's conclusions will be discussed below).

But in fact one of the most salient features of Plautine comedy is a pronounced and heavily biased sociopolitical content.

Plautus was, in his own way, no less concerned with his contemporary world than had been Aristophanes.

In order for this claim to be made, some illusions must first be dispelled. One of these has to do with the fact that Plautus ostensibly functioned as a translator. The settings of his plays, and the characters with which they are peopled, are invariably Greek, not Roman. The social institutions and relationships they describe, and therefore also (the reader might care to think) the feeling-tones associated with this ostensible setting, are likewise Greek. Hence, to put this argument in its most extreme form, Plautus may have been a humble translator who was entirely unaware of any social or political content in his plays or of any possible resonance between the Greek world they fictionally portray and the actual Roman world in which they were produced.

An explanation of this sort is doubtless what Plautus himself, with wide-eyed innocence, would have offered for the benefit of Roman censorship authorities. But in fact, for a variety of reasons, it is impossibly naïve. Even if his plays were merely translations of Greek New Comedies (and they are not) they are nonetheless Roman cultural artifacts. In reading them we must always make room for the possibility that, like any other cultural artifacts injected into a foreign context, they could acquire meanings quite different than those intended by the authors of their Greek prototypes, and also that they could elicit different emotional responses from Roman spectators. This would be true automatically, by dint of their very translation into Latin and production in that language, without reference to the translator's personal intentions. If, for example, you translate the Greek word for "mother" as *matrona* or the Greek word for "marketplace" as *forum*, whether you mean to or not, you are introducing a specific Roman coloration.

Then too, if these plays were mere translations, it would still be true that their translator had the ability to choose which Greek originals to appropriate, since he had a wide selection at his disposal. This in itself created an important avenue for the intrusion of the translator's personal predilections.

But of course the understanding that these plays are mere translations is impossible to maintain, and any attempt to relegate Plautus to the role of a translator, merely "sharking up" scripts so his theater troupe had material with which to work, is unrealistic. His plays are very adroit, and quite individualistic, adaptations. In this sense, they are as original artistic creations as are, say, Shakespeare's adapted versions of his plays and those of Terence. Signs of artistic autonomy abound. By the practice of *contaminatio* Plautus makes plots longer and more complex, by adding elements drawn from other Greek New Comedies. He supplies song and dance, elements wholly missing from his models. He adds energy, zest, earthiness, and occasional ribaldry to their sometimes quite prosaic diction. His plays are, in short, much funnier, often in a distinctly farcical way. Some of the spirit and possibly some of the more specific features may be borrowed from native Italian comic forms with peasant origins, such as Atellan Farce, about which we unfortunately know very little. The Romans were beginning to find their way to the city in larger numbers, but were not far removed from the farm. There is much in Plautus calculated to appeal to the earthy tastes of the Italian peasant.

Plautus frequently adds Romanizing detail to tip the wink to the audience that the fiction of these plays' Greek settings need not be taken overseriously. They may be read as genuinely Roman works, and there is no *a priori* reason for doubting that Plautus was well aware of the social and political implications of what he was doing.

In order to discuss these implications, we must consider the specific nature of the society in which Plautus' plays were produced. Roman society was not only characterized by a well-defined class structure, featuring a small and dominant elite despite its ostensibly republican nature. A cultural anthropologist would be equally if not more impressed by another and more idiosyncratic feature of Roman society: its very pronounced patriarchal nature.

In contemporary feminist vocabulary "patriarchal" has been co-opted as a broad-gauge synonym for "male-dominated." But here I am using this word in its original etymological sense: Rome was a society presided over, not just by men, but more precisely by fathers and by fatherlike old men. The dominating figure in Roman society was the *paterfamilias*, the male head of the household or *familia*, who occupied this position by dint of his seniority. And the *familia* was bound together by ties of upward-directed loyalty and duty (summarized by the word *pietas*), far more than by the bonds of mutual affection characteristic of the modern nuclear family. Indeed, at least in theory, the *paterfamilias* had the power of life and death over all the members of the *familia*. Even if social pressures kept them from exercising this degree of power, every Roman would have known tales of fathers doing just this from the semimythical realm of early national history (cf. Livy 8.7ff.). On the political level, the dominant institution was the Senate, the assembly of senior males (*senex* means "old man"), which can be regarded as a corporation of the heads of important *familiae*. Not for nothing were the members of the Senate designated the "fathers" (*patres conscripti*). Therefore *pietas* was not only the glue that held together the individual *familia*; it also acquired wider political significance.

The duration of the authority exercised by the *paterfamilias* was equally unusual. We live in a society in which individuals are freed—and many experience this as a genuine liberation—upon reaching adulthood. Not so in Plautus' Rome. A male member of a *familia* remained in a fixed and unchanging relation to his *paterfamilias* as long as the latter lived: such a male aged 40 would stand in precisely the same relation to his 60-year-old father as he stood at 20 to his 40-year-old father.

The specific degree and nature of intergenerational tension presumably varies from one male-dominated society to the next in direct proportion to the authoritarian sway exerted by senior men. Therefore, in view of the extremely patriarchal nature of Roman society, we may assume that the degree of such tensions within this society must have been extraordinarily high, more so than, for example, within Greek society, which was equally male-dominated, but not equally patriarchal. The existence of attendant chafing psychological tensions and frustrations must have been one of the predominant features of the Roman male psyche.

The kind of psychological interpretation pioneered by Sigmund Freud works very well when applied to Plautine comedy. Freud himself operated in a paternalistic and repressive culture, and he was probably wrong to jump to the conclusion that the kind of psychological problems he found endemic in members of such a society have a universal human validity. But Roman society was so markedly paternalistic and authoritarian that it must have created a roughly similar psychological environment.

When one reads Plautine comedy one sees that it very typically deals not just with family affairs but with humorous representations of power struggles within families. These struggles take many forms, but none is commoner than that between males of different generations within the household, most frequently between sons and their fathers.

That this is a characteristically Plautine theme is suggested by the one instance in which we are privileged to compare a Greek original with Plautus' adaptation thereof.[4] First, this is Sostratus' soliloquy from the third act of Menander, *Dis Exapaton* (92ff.). The dramatic situation is that young Sostratus has been sent abroad by his father with some money to repay a debt. Instead, he falls in love with a girl and, with the help of his friend Moschus, wants to keep the money to purchase the girl's freedom. He wrongly gets the idea that Moschus and the girl are double-crossing him:[5]

> And now that my pockets are empty, I think I'd like to see my fine ladylove making up to me, and expecting—"this instant," she says to herself—all the cash I'm carrying. "For he's got it all right, and he's certainly generous—the very best—and I've earned it." With her fine foot-work, she's certainly turned out to be just what I once thought she was. But Moschus is a fool, and I'm sorry for him; I'm furious with him, and yet I don't altogether blame him for letting me down; it's *her*, the bold piece.

In Mnesilochus' speech in Plautus' *Bacchides* (500ff.), Plautus turns this into:

> I simply don't know which of them to think is now my worse enemy, my old friend or Bacchis. Wanted him instead of me, did she? She can have him! That's fine. But I tell you this, she'll certainly pay for what she's done. Heaven help me, if I don't absolutely and completely—love her. I'll make sure she won't say she's found someone to laugh at: I'll go straight home and—rob my father. What I steal, I'll—give to her. Oh, I'll get my own back on her in all sorts of ways. I'll press her so hard that there'll be beggary—for my father. But I must be clean out of my mind, maundering on like this about what's going to happen. God! I'm in love, I think—as if I didn't know. But she'll never be a fraction of a feather's weight heavier from my money. I'll

be the most beggarly beggar before that. Never, I assure you, never in her life will she make a fool of me. I've made up my mind: I'll pay over every penny to my father, this minute. So she'll be making up to me when my pockets are empty and I haven't a penny, when it'll have no more effect than if she were prattling away at a dead man's grave. I've quite made up my mind to hand the money over to my father: that's final. When I do, I'll ask him, as a favour to me, to let Chrysalus off, and not be angry with him for fooling him over the money. He did it for me, and it's only fair that I should look after him, when it was to help me that he made up this story.

Plautus has introduced quite a number of changes, none more striking than that the material about Mnesilochus' impulse to cheat his father is added by him to reinforce the importance of this theme in the play. To be sure, in *Bacchides* Mnesilochus overcomes his initial impulse to bankrupt his father (in some other Plautine plays, such as *Mostellaria*, the son is not so self-disciplined). Nevertheless, the theme of father-son relationships seems to be given extra stress by Plautus, the specter of intergenerational conflict is raised, and the possibility of filial rebellion is in the air.

Given the specific nature of Roman society, it is impossible that the representations of male generational disputes could not have acquired major social implications and also have played upon very powerful feelings in the audience. We have already seen that there are a couple of false attitudes one might adopt that would have the effect of obscuring this essential fact. One might be misled by the ostensible Greekness of these plays. Or one could take the Freudian line that, since the internalized Oedipal drama is an essential component of the universal givenness of the male psyche, stories that play on this nuclear situation have no essentially different meaning from one society to the next. The remarks made above should suffice to dispel both illusions. Whatever the sociopolitical implications of such representations may have been in their original Greek contexts, when translated into Latin these implications must have been considerably altered or at least intensified.

But the formulation just given of the centrality of disputes and power struggles between sons and their fathers (or between youngsters and other stern old men or agents of patriarchal authority in some more generalized sense) is incomplete. The issue is not just the fact that Plautus represents such conflicts. More to the point is the attitude he invariably adopts toward the situations he portrays: sympathy is always placed on the side of the son rebelling against his father, or of youth rebelling against old age. Sons and their hedonistic enterprises are portrayed in a tolerant or favorable light; fathers and their authoritarian values are not.

In all three Plautine plays we shall be examining, Plautus adds various Romanizing touches to remind the spectator that the fathers in his plays may be ostensibly Greek but actually embody features specifically characteristic of the Roman *paterfamilias*. Put in the most simplistic terms, his favorite tactic is to portray his comic fathers as unsympathetic agelasts. He lovingly explores their weak or unpleasant traits so as to point up major discrepancies between what they should be and what they actually are. This discrepancy can be regarded as a form of hypocrisy. His father–son plays regularly end with fathers' defeats and humiliations. The net effect is to damage the prestigious mystique of the *paterfamilias*. More broadly, in Plautine comedy we find a sustained assault on the values of patriarchy: on puritanism, the work ethic, *pietas*, and all the rest of the ideological machinery supportive of patriarchal authority. This assault, moreover, is part of a more general attack on authoritarianism. Plautus represents other forms of confrontation or power struggle within the *familia* (unconvincingly disguised as its Greek equivalent, the *oikos*), notably contention between its servile and free members and the battle between the sexes. Indeed, in some of his plays he goes so far as to attack the institution of the *familia* itself. He shows how it is, or at least can be, an inhumane and unjust institution that exploits its subordinate members. Under such conditions, the upward-directed loyalty of *pietas* begins to look like a form of slave mentality. This is shown, for example, in *Asinaria*, where the son allows his father to exploit him out of a sense of *pietas*. In looking at the *familia* and its attendant ideology, Plautus regularly sides with the underdog and the values he or she represents.

So it looks very much as if Plautine comedy conducts a sustained and programmatic assault on Roman authoritarianism and its ideological supports. This assault, and its corresponding subversive attitude, is scarcely subtle and Plautus makes no great effort to disguise it. Why, therefore, has it gone unappreciated, or at least severely underappreciated, even by Plautus' most outspoken admirers?

The answer lies in some further contemporary illusions about the nature of ancient comedy that must now be cleared up. There exists a common understanding that the world of comedy is a festival situation somehow disconnected from that of actual life. One of the most sensitive, intelligent, and influential fulllength studies of Plautine comedy available is Erich Segal's *Roman Laughter*.[6] Segal's conclusion was that Roman comedy provided "a holiday for the superego" (196), a temporary opportunity to "escape the toga" (197). Then, according to his final sentence, the spectators "leave the play and return to their own *negotium*, the business of being Roman." Remarks like this seem to presume a sort of impenetrable barrier between the world of the comic stage and that of reality. To be sure, the world of comedy is a safe one where threats are not to be taken seriously and where genuine pain does not exist. But this does not necessarily mean that the spectator forgets what he feels and knows about real life when he comes to the theater, or that he will not remember what he has felt and learned while watching comedy after he goes home. Additionally, although Segal takes an approach modeled on that of C. L. Barber, he pays no attention to Barber's observation (quoted here in an earlier context) about the disruptive potential of festive comedy.

The position taken here is based on the assumption that comedy no less than serious drama, and popular entertainment no less than high art, can perform a deliberately instructive role. Greek Old Comedy was performed in a festival context and, as embodied in the plays of Aristophanes, bears profound marks of its festive roots. But this scarcely kept Aristophanes from becoming seriously engaged with the issues of everyday reality, since the universe of the festival and the universe of everyday life turn out not to be entirely disjunct: what would be the point of his editorializing about contemporary political, social, and cultural matters if they were? What right do we have to assume on *a priori* grounds that the situation must have been different for Plautus?

A somewhat more sophisticated misconception is founded on some modern attempts at developing theories of comic catharsis, based on the claim that comedy arouses certain emotions in order to purge them by exerting some kind of homeopathic effect. One could invoke this notion in order to suggest that Plautine comedy plays on the kind of resentments, frustrations, and hostilities engendered in the underdog spectator by his confrontations with authority in order to produce a catharsis ridding the spectator of such feelings. This line of thinking, carried to its logical extreme, might even lead to the perverse conclusion that Plautus' comedies look ostensibly subversive but are in fact instruments of authoritarian social control (variants of this social-utilitarian theory of comedy have been repeatedly advanced by modern critics).[7] When applied to actual cases such a theory can produce some marvelous conclusions: did Aristophanes lampoon Cleon in order to strengthen his hold on Athens? But surely it is possible to suggest a quite different theory of comic catharsis. If somebody swallows a poison by mistake, he is administered an emetic in order to purge himself of the poison. The poison that comic catharsis purges us of is not our hostilities toward dominant authority, but rather the feelings of inferiority, intimidation, and guilt that these authorities engender in us, and that are important instruments of their control. The object of comic catharsis, coupled with comic belittlement of authority figures, is far more likely to weaken their power over us than to strengthen it.

Plautus' thematic assault on authoritarianism generally has personal psychological implications—we shall observe distinctly Oedipal features in his plays—and also social ones. And as has already been suggested, his plays and their collective message also have more specific implications for the immediate historical situation in which they were written.

For Plautus was writing against the background of a protracted conflict between supporters of traditional Roman values and admirers of the more liberal and humane values of the Hellenized cosmopolitan civilization spread throughout the Mediterranean basin into which Rome was rapidly emerging; and his plays can be read as signs that he himself was an active participant in this struggle.

The conquest of Greek city-states in Magna Graecia, Sicily, and the Greek mainland opened Roman eyes to the existence of a vast, cosmopolitan outside world. Foreigners made their way to Rome freely or as slaves; in either case they brought their cultural baggage with them. Some such slaves were pressed into service as teachers of Roman youth. The most memorable example of this phenomenon is the Greek slave-schoolmaster Livius Andronicus, who translated the *Odyssey* into Latin and afterward translated and produced Greek tragedies and comedies, thereby founding both Latin literature and Roman drama. Imported Greeks also served as doctors and filled other needs for technical expertise. Roman victories led to prosperity on a scale heretofore unimagined and created a market for art, literature, entertainment, and all the other appurtenances of a leisure class (this process is described by Livy 39.6.3ff.). The result of these developments was that in countless ways foreign influences spread through all levels of Roman society, and there was now an upper class with time and money on its hands that was particularly receptive to Hellenistic influence.

But the introduction of such values evoked a trend of reactionary repression, and the failure of such attempts to stifle or at least impose severe limits on such borrowing was fateful for determining the shape ultimately assumed by Roman civilization and the nature of its culture.

The story of this clash of Roman and foreign values in the second century B.C. has been extensively told elsewhere.[8] Here a few highlights of the struggle may be mentioned. In 186 B.C. the Senate voted to quash the introduction of the Dionysiac religion (Livy 39.7ff. and *C.I.L.* I^2 581, the *Senatusconsultum de Bacchanalibus*). Similarly, in 161 B.C. it made a decision to banish Greek philosophers and rhetoricians as unwholesome influences (Suetonius, *Orat.* 1). In 139 B.C. Jews and astrologers were likewise exiled and, if our evidence is to be trusted, we even hear of an unsuccessful attempt to banish dramatic performances as late as 115 B.C. (Cassiodorus, *Chron.*, year 639).

The leading spokesman for native, traditional Roman values and greatest opponent of the introduction of Greek culture and learning was Cato the Elder (234–149 B.C.), whose attitude on this score is thoroughly documented by Plutarch in his *Life of Cato* (cf. especially chapters 22f., and also Pliny, *Natural History* 1.12f.). Both in his public and private capacities Cato tried to exhibit himself as a champion and living model of the *mos maiorum*, or traditional Roman way of life, and in his capacity as Censor he tried to stem the tide of Hellenism that, as he saw it, was inundating Rome. Insofar as his political archenemies, the younger Scipio Africanus and his circle of friends, were enlightened philhellenes, the clash of traditional Roman values versus newly introduced Greek ones became caught up in the party politics of the time.[9] To be sure, Cato only assumed his Censorship in the year of Plautus' death, but the issue had been brewing for some time, as exemplified by the clash caused by the Senate's reaction to the introduction of Dionysus' cult in 186 B.C.

Literature seems to have been caught up in that particular dispute. Livy gives a long account of how the Senate became aware of the importation of the organized worship of Dionysus. Various allegations of sexual and other forms of misconduct were made that seemed sufficiently lurid that the Senate issued a quite draconian decree forbidding five or more people to assemble in connection with this cult, setting other severe limitations, and threatening death as the penalty for noncompliance. Aeschylus' *The Edonians* seems to have been a play similar in its content to Euripides' later *The Bacchae*, which narrated the Thracian king Lycurgus' opposition to the coming of Dionysus and his consequent downfall. This tragedy seems to have been translated under the title *Lycurgus* by Naevius, and the attractive suggestion has been made (by Agostino Pastorino)[10] that this play was translated and produced while the problem of Dionysiac religion at Rome was a live issue. If so, the unfriendly equation Senate = Lycurgus could readily be drawn, and by the mere dint of its translation this Greek play would acquire the character of a critical commentary on a contemporary subject.

In much the same way, you can take Mommsen's moralizing criticisms of Roman comedy and rephrase them in a more illuminating way. Roman comedy served as a vehicle transmitting the more liberal and humane values of Hellenism, giving frequent unfavorable representations of ostensibly Greek equivalents of traditional Roman authoritarianism, severity, legal-mindedness, and similar aspects of the *mos maiorum*. Certainly there was an admixture of hedonism in these new Hellenic values, but it would be wrong to focus attention on the part to the exclusion of the whole. What is being aggressively preached is not hedonism so much as *humanitas*. The special importance of comedy as such a vehicle comes from the circumstances under which it was produced: not for any kind of social or intellectual elite, but openly and for free in the Forum, available for seeing and hearing by the entire Roman populace. Plautus kept up a steady and highly visible barrage of what might be called anti-Catonism. If he did so, who is to deny that subversive attack was not his intention?

Plautus himself, like most of the other writers of Roman comedy, was a down-and-outer recruited from the lower orders of society, and he is supposed to have spent part of his life in slavery as the reward for bankruptcy. Having this personal history, he had little reason to love traditional Roman authoritarian paternalism and its values. A sustained subversive attack on Roman paternalism, unconvincingly disguised under an outward veneer of Greek settings, lies at heart of his comic art and supplies it with much of its energy and verve. Far from being a philosophically detached observer of human foibles, in the mode of Terence, he is distinguished by his engaged commitment in representing disputes, power struggles, and clashes of values, and he is scarcely bashful in showing where his sympathies lie. Nor is there any reason to doubt that he, no less than Aristophanes, is trying to arouse, instruct, and inculcate similar attitudes in his audience.

On the basis of these reflections, it seems advisable to discourage a way of reading Plautus that relies overmuch on psychological considerations. When we turn to his plays, it will quickly become evident that we are fishing in some very Freudian waters indeed. For the critic willing to pay attention to this mode of interpretation, the strong Oedipal overtones in these plays will be apparent. Comedy's laughter undoubtedly has a cathartic effect. Laughter purges us of tensions and anxieties, especially when it is directed against the comic equivalents of the sources of such bad feelings. So the possibility can scarcely be denied that one purpose of Plautine comedy may have been to purge the theatergoer of his Oedipal anxieties. But it is impossible to believe that this is the whole story, in view of the heavy societal implications of his plays. For in them the tension between fathers and sons is not merely the dramatization of some inner psychic melodrama. Such situations allude to concrete social realities. In this sense, therefore, Freud's Oedipal situation is itself really only a metaphor, although a highly significant one, which served to mobilize the spectator's hostilities and frustrations and direct them against the *paterfamilias* figure. The tension created as one generation thrusts upward and begins to think of displacing its predecessor is a very real fact. By combining stories about generational conflicts within single families with the conflict of Hellenistic values versus those of Roman forefathers—for that is what *mos maiorum* literally means—Plautus transforms what would otherwise be abstract tales about the eternal human condition within families into creations of considerable immediacy for the time and place in which they were written.

Mostellaria

Mostellaria ("*The Haunted House*") is based on the play *Phasma* ("*The Ghost*") by the New Comedy poet Philemon. It begins with an acrimonious scene between two slaves, Grumio and Tranio, belonging to a master named Theopropides. Grumio is a slave from his rural estates, while Tranio works in his city home. Grumio is highly indignant because in the master's absence Tranio has been squandering his goods. Worse yet, he has been corrupting their master's son Philolaches, egging him on in his career of riotous living: drunk all the time, feasting, supporting parasites, buying slave girls their freedom, in general carrying on with his cronies like so many Greeks (22 and 64). He predicts dire consequences for Tranio, enumerating some of the punishments that await him, such as being dragged off to the country and placed on a labor gang, or even crucifixion. Tranio responds to this grumpy onslaught with *sang-froid*. All this drinking, loving, and whoring is his own affair. He is risking his own neck, not Grumio's. Come to think of it, Grumio, you reek of garlic, you stinking clodhopper. Aren't there some cows that need tending back on the farm? He sweeps off, leaving Grumio expostulating. Theopropides has been gone three years, and he hopes the master will return before all his estate is sent to rack and ruin.

The comic introduction consisting of a dialogue between slaves is a traditional device, found as early as such Aristophanic plays as *The Knights* and *The Wasps*. This one accomplishes more than informing the audience about the narrative's background and introducing the important character Tranio. It also limns the basic polarity that organizes the whole play. It plays off hedonism against the work ethic and the fun-loving against the dour, and if Grumio can scarcely be said to be an authority figure, he certainly is free in invoking authority's machinery of punishment in support of his values. Plautus firmly locates the former values and kinds of people in the city and the latter in the countryside.

Tranio exits and Philolaches enters, immediately launching into a remarkable extended address to the audience (84ff.). He's been thinking things over and has come to the conclusion that a man is very like a building. Even if its builder constructs it carefully, when its occupants neglect its upkeep it will deteriorate and finally collapse. Same with himself. He received a careful upbringing, but fell into profligate ways. Now his money, his credit, reputation, virtue, and prestige are shot to hell. "I don't seem to be able to repair my house before the whole thing falls down in total ruin, foundation and all, and nobody can help me. I'm heartsick when I see what I am now and what I used to be" (147–9). His conclusion: "I'm good for nothing, and I see I've been made this way by my own inner nature" (156). The boy is well aware that he is doing wrong, but admits that he is helpless to resist because he is bound to obey the imperatives of his innate nature or character (*ingenium*).

This soliloquy, however, leads nowhere. Philolaches may be aware of his shortcomings but, perhaps because he is using his final conclusion as an excuse, he is really unrepentant and has no intention of reforming. And even by the end of the play there is no indication that he will change his profligate ways.

Next follows a long scene in which Philolaches' girl friend Philematum converses with her maidservant Scapha with Philolaches overhearing and offering a running commentary. Scapha is urging Philematum to take a cynical attitude and spread her favors around, but Philolaches has purchased Philematum's freedom and so she feels she must show her gratitude by remaining loyal to the boy. Philolaches, overhearing, is thrilled. A couple of his remarks deserve to be singled out. When Philematum and Scapha are discussing the need for her financial support, Philolaches exclaims that he will sell his father into slavery before he will see her impoverished (229f.). When the girl expresses her gratitude to him, he goes even further (233f.): "would that my father's death would be reported to me right

now, so that I might disinherit myself and make her his heir!"
Here we have the same son's hope touched upon (in characteristically inverted form) by Philocleon near the end of *The Wasps*,
that the father's death will leave the son with sufficient money
to lavish on his love affairs.

After this scene is over, a boon blade named Callidamates
comes reeling drunkenly up to Philolaches' house, accompanied
by his own mistress. After a little byplay he unabashedly collaps-
es on a handy couch and passes out. Thus ends Act I.

Act II begins on a very much more agitated note. Tranio bursts
in and, in horror, announces some catastrophic news to the audience: he has just seen old man Theopropides down at the har-
bor. All is lost! He himself is bound for ruin. Anybody in the
audience want to be paid to be crucified in his place? Guess not.
Philolaches appears, hears the news, and is reduced to a helpless
state of shock. Callidamates had better be woken up and
removed. When he has been shaken awake, he sits up and cheerfully offers to murder the old man (384). The offer is refused and
he is hustled into the house.

Faced with Philolaches' panicky despair, Tranio takes charge.
He has a plan, whereby Theopropides will not only refuse to
enter the house but will also flee far away. The only thing
Philolaches and his friends have to do is shut themselves up
inside and not make a sound. They should all place their trust in
him: a tricky business like this needs the management of an
experienced man, a man who can make everything turn out
right without landing himself in the soup (408ff.).

The preparations are quickly made and Theopropides soon
appears. His first words are a prayer of gratitude to Neptune for
sparing his life during his voyage. Tranio, overhearing, offers his
own running commentary: "By god, Neptune, you've made a
huge mistake, missing such a grand opportunity" (438f.). Theopropides imagines his homecoming will be welcome. Again,
Tranio: "By heaven, the man who came to announce your death
would be a great deal more welcome!" (442f.). Then the two men
confront each other. The old man wants to go in the house, but
Tranio reacts with horror. He spins a complicated and fantastic
story about how in Theopropides' absence it was discovered that
the house is haunted because of a murder once having been
committed in it. Therefore the house has been boarded up. This

fiction manages to play on Theopropides' superstitious side, and he is quickly infected by Tranio's spurious sense of dread, much to the slave's secret delight.

So far, so good, but when comic deceptions of this sort are woven, unforeseen complications are bound to arise that all but ruin the deceiver's scheme. In the present instance, an indignant moneylender named Misargyrides unexpectedly turns up demanding repayment for all the money he has lent Philolaches. Theopropides is puzzled by this, especially when he learns of the enormous debt that his son has run up. When Tranio urges him to settle the debt, he asks the inevitable embarrassing question: for what purpose was the money borrowed? On the spur of the moment, Tranio comes up with the answer that Philolaches borrowed it to raise the down payment on a new house. After all, since the old one proved to be haunted, a new one was necessary. Theopropides is pleased by this sensible purchase, but asks another inevitable and equally awkward question: precisely where is this house? For he would very much like to inspect it.

Tranio is once more thrown back on his inventive resources. In desperation he points to the house of their next-door neighbor. Theopropides naturally wants to go inside, provoking yet another crisis. Fortunately Tranio is able to stall Theopropides by saying that the women within must have the chance to get ready for the entry, and so the old man is hustled off the stage long enough for Tranio to collect his wits.

By a stroke of good luck, at this point the owner of the house next door appears. This is Simo, another old man but cut from entirely different cloth than Theopropides. We first meet him sneaking out of his house. His wife has given him a wonderful lunch and now wants him to go to bed. So he is going off to the Forum. From the insistence with which this issue of his going to bed is mentioned throughout his monologue and his extreme repugnance at the idea, it is evident that he is really avoiding her sexual advances: "the old hag wanted to drag me off to the bedroom!" (696). Tranio overhears and commiserates. But then he has a bright idea and engages Simo in conversation. The old man asks if the usual goings-on are still happening in the house, and he adds that he thoroughly approves: "indulge yourself—think how short life is" (724f.).

Tranio reveals the terrible news of Theopropides' return, and Simo sympathizes. He immediately recognizes the danger facing Tranio. First he will receive a whipping. Then irons await him, and finally the cross (743f.). The slave pretends to be terror-stricken, falling at Simo's knees and begging for help. Then he launches into another of his lies. Theopropides has decided to add women's quarters to his house, looking forward to the time his son marries. His architect greatly admires Simo's house and has proposed it as a model. Would it be possible for Theopropides to inspect the building? Simo genially agrees.

So Tranio goes to fetch Theopropides. As he crosses the stage from the one house to the other, he delivers himself of a crowing monologue in which he brags about his control over these two old men. "Muleteers have their pack-mules, but I have pack-men, and they're really laden down—they'll carry whatever you load 'em with" (780–2). As he escorts Theopropides back across the stage he carefully prepares him. That old gentleman you see is the individual who sold the house to Philolaches. Now he deeply regrets having done so. This bit of misinformation allows Tranio to glide over some rough spots. For example, when Simo cheerfully invites Theopropides to look the house over "as if it were your own," Theopropides naturally asks Tranio what this "as if" is about, and Tranio is able to explain that away in terms of Simo's alleged regret over its sale.

In the course of the house inspection, Tranio solemnly points out a picture in the portico. The two old men cannot see it, so the slave is so good as to describe it (832ff.): a crow stands between two vultures and is pecking at the both of them in turns. Since they still can't see it, he is even more specific: "look in my direction, then you'll see the crow—and if you can't make it out, then look in your own direction and perhaps you'll see the vultures" (835ff.).

Act IV begins with a monologue, by Callidamates' philosophical slave Phaniscus (858ff.). He reflects on a slave's lot. Some slaves grow to fear nothing. Then they fall into bad ways and earn nothing but whippings. His own plan is to build his life on the principle of not getting whipped, and therefore he sticks to the good old straight and narrow. After all, a master's only what his slaves make him. If they're good, so is he. If they are rascals, he becomes one himself. In the present instance, all of Callidamates' other slaves were too lazy to go fetch their master, so he is undertaking the task by himself—won't they be in for a scourging when Master returns!

Theopropides and Tranio emerge from Simo's house. Theopropides is overjoyed about the supposed purchase and is eager to pay off the moneylender. No problem, says Tranio; just give me the money and I'll make sure he gets it. When Theopropides gets a bit suspicious, he blandly asks "would I dare play a trick on you in word or deed?...Since I came into your service have I ever deceived you?" (924, 926).

Phaniscus and another slave of Callidamates reappear in order to retrieve their master. When they start knocking on the door Theopropides is puzzled and enters into conversation with Phaniscus. They are unaware of Theopropides' identity and so innocently reveal the truth to the old man, informing him of all the loose living that has gone on in the house during his absence and supplying some lurid details of his son's dissipation. And he also reveals that one slave in particular has distinguished himself by his misdeeds, a man named Tranio. Won't Philolaches' father be aghast when he comes home and finds out about all this roistering!

Theopropides indeed is aghast, and matters grow even worse because as soon as Phaniscus disappears Simo arrives and, after some humorous dialogue as they talk at cross-purposes, the two old men compare notes and figure out how they have been swindled by Tranio. At the end of Act IV Theopropides howls that he has been ruined. All he can think of is revenge, so he asks Simo if he can borrow some whips. Genial as ever, Simo agrees.

Act V has to do with the impending punishment of Tranio. When he sees Theopropides standing in front of the house waiting for him, Tranio realizes that the jig is up. Nevertheless he has sufficient confidence in his cleverness that he is not unduly perturbed. He knows that Theopropides has decided to feign ignorance and so he plays along. When the old man innocently informs him that Simo has denied receiving any money for his house, he pretends surprise. Theopropides claims that Simo has agreed to let him have all his slaves in order to be put to the question about the missing money (1086)—yet another reference to the torture of slaves, because this is the only way in which slave testimony could be taken under Roman law—and so Tranio proposes to help him wait. But as they continue their conversation he sits on a handy altar in mock-innocence. Theopropides, with equally fake innocence, tries to cajole him off the altar, but he politely refuses. Thus, when pretenses are dropped, he is in a place of sanctuary and beyond his master's reach. So when Theopropides begins ranting at him, he can jeer back from a position of security. Theopropides promises condign punishments, but Tranio continues to mock him for the fool he is.

The impasse is broken by the entrance of Callidamates. Newly sober, he has come as a representative of Philolaches and his pals. In the most urbane way he tries to calm Theopropides. At first to no avail: master and slave continue their mutual threats and jeers until Callidamates reveals that Philolaches' friends have managed to scrape together enough money to make a full restitution. This news produces the desired change of attitude. At first Theopropides is reluctant to let Tranio off the hook, but the slave says he is sorry and points out that if his master forgives the crimes he has committed today, then he can doubly punish him for those he will undoubtedly commit tomorrow. Theopropides relents and the play comes to an abrupt end.

It would be possible to imagine a cheerful and straightforward play in which a series of practical jokes are played on a father so that a son might enjoy his ladylove. But *Mostellaria* is not quite that play. Two elements serve to darken and complicate its tone. During the course of the play Theopropides' death is repeatedly hoped for, and this wish is placed in the mouths of no less than three characters. And repeated allusions to crucifixion and the similar horrors that await a disobedient slave serve to raise the stakes by reminding the audience of the very genuine perils involved in Tranio's self-imposed tightrope act. The presence of both of these elements entitle the reader to wonder what precisely is going on.

Mostellaria seems susceptible to two readings, each by itself inadequate, but neither excluding the possibility or diminishing the value of the other. First, one can apply a psychological interpretation. We shall see a distinctly Oedipal undercurrent in *Asinaria* and *Casina*, where sons and fathers are competing for the same woman. In the case of *Mostellaria* and plays with similar plots, it would seem possible to carry the argument a step farther. In *Mostellaria* father and son are scarcely in competition for an erotic object, but one can argue that in any play where a father stands between a son and the fulfillment of his erotic ambitions, and where the father is therefore cast in the role of an obstacle that must be circumvented or defeated, we are really confronted with a plot in which the Oedipal situation is disguised by displacement but is nonetheless hovering in the background.[11]

The usefulness of this suggestion lies in its explanatory power. Such a reading renders fully understandable Philolaches' openly expressed wish for the death of his father, and similar hopes placed in the mouths of Callidamates and Tranio are then seen as the son's wish displaced onto other characters. Furthermore, this suggestion perhaps makes Tranio's motivation more comprehensible.

For one must wonder exactly why Tranio is willing to launch on the complicated and risky business of trying to fool his master, and why he goes about the job with such relish. A partial reason is of course supplied by the speech he makes when he first learns of Theopropides' return (348ff.): in his master's absence he has been playing the rascal and so he has every reason to fear imminent retribution. But when Tranio and Philolaches collide shortly thereafter and he agrees to help the boy (388ff.), this motivation goes unmentioned, and we never hear of it again except when Tranio alludes to it as a device for playing on Simo's sympathies. Certainly, Tranio is not Zero Mostel, and in view of the popularity of *A Funny Thing Happened on the Way to the Forum* it is worth bearing in mind that the ambition of the clever Plautine slave of the Tranio–Pseudolus type is not usually to gain his manumission. Rather, it appears that Tranio's major motivation is clever deception for the pure joy of it. He seems to act out of the uncomplicated pleasure of demonstrating his intelligence and general superiority and taking advantage of his master's foolish gullibility. Certainly his self-satisfied asides and monologues and his phoney "painting" of the highly symbolic crow and vultures show the fun he has in manipulating and outthinking his supposed betters. Everything he does is calculated to show that he is the better man.

But a psychological reading points to a deeper understanding of such slaves' motivations. In a recent article, Holt Parker has suggested:

> The Plautine *adulescens* is naïve in his monomaniac pursuit of the girl. He has no inhibitions at all, and we in the audience can enjoy vicariously his evil wishes against his father and his ultimate triumph, while protected from guilt by our own sense of superiority. Likewise, the Plautine *servus* is monomaniac in his pursuit of trickery as an end in itself. He too has no inhibitions, and we vicariously enjoy his evil deeds against the father....However, it is the impudent slave who allows the youth to be naïve, by removing the intentionality. It is the slave who acts, plans, intends, does, and so takes on (and takes away) all the guilt that would have fallen on the son.[12]

So, according to a Freudian reduction of the dramatic situation to the level of Oedipal psychodrama, important components of the Oedipal son's personality are displaced onto Tranio. Because of his ridiculous and slavelike nature he is able to translate into action the son's inmost wishes. For a Freudian interpreter, at any rate, a sort of "proof" that such a projection is occurring lies in the fact that Tranio too gives voice to Philolaches' wish that Theopropides might die. Such a psychological understanding that the son's expected intentionality and guilt are not really absent, but are merely displaced, serves to explain the extreme passivity and strange helplessness of Philolaches and similar comic sons.

A notorious characteristic of "clever slave" plays is that this type of slave dominates, and that the upper-class youths on whose behalf they intervene are eternally passive and feckless. This slave is the cleverest, most adventurous, and most dynamic character in the repertoire of New Comedy characters, and his scheming serves to drive the plot. The psychological interpretation proposed here provides a theoretical explanation both of the slaves' dynamism and of the young men's passivity. The element of displacement also makes the play less censorable and more acceptable to the audience.

By the same token, part of the Oedipal son's personality is also displaced onto Callidamates. Like Tranio, he can speak and act in ways that Philolaches cannot. While Philolaches can only wistfully hope for Theopropides' death, Callidamates proposes to translate this desire into bold action. If Tranio embodies the Oedipal son's dynamism, Callidamates represents his aggressive side. This too has the effect of shifting the burden of guilt away from the son. And again, if the audience is protected from feelings of guilt vis-à-vis the slave Tranio out of a sense of superiority, Callidamates' extreme drunkenness serves to engender a similar sense in the spectator.

This interpretation of Tranio's function renders explicable one of the play's most striking peculiarities, the complete disappearance of Philolaches before the play is even half over. Tranio volunteers to help Philolaches even though the boy does not ask for his assistance, and Philolaches places himself completely in the slave's hands. His exit line in this scene (407) consists of the significant words "I place myself and my hopes in your custody, Tranio." Then he vanishes.

In accordance with comic convention, the play must end with a reconciliation. Since *Mostellaria* is about a boy's rebellion against his father, one would predict that Philolaches would appear again at play's end, and that the essential reconciliation to be effected would be that of Philolaches and Theopropides. Rather remarkably, therefore, the reconciliation achieved in Act V is between Tranio, Callidamates, and Theopropides. Philolaches, to be sure, is mentioned, but he does not appear, and the final resolution of the play consists of Theopropides' at least temporary forgiveness of Tranio. If we are to think that on a deep psychological level Tranio and Callidamates embody the Oedipal son's dynamic and aggressive side, then the inner logic of the play's reconciliation becomes comprehensible. Indeed, according to this logic, a reconciliation that merely occurred between father and son would not be fully satisfactory since this would not embrace a reconciliation between the father and the son's more aggressive aspects, personified by other characters.

One might expect that the conclusion of the play would feature some sort of change of heart in Philolaches that would resolve the issue of his awareness of his malfeasances expressed in the monologue delivered as we first meet him. This long speech contains at least the germ of a repentant attitude, which Plautus could have built upon later in the play. As it stands, the monologue is really only a kind of red herring: it is a sign pointing nowhere, and it raises expectations that are left unfulfilled. As the play stands this speech (perhaps inherited from Plautus' Greek original) is its main weakness. It seems intrusive, and Plautus might have been well advised if he had eliminated it.

The same kind of psychologizing interpretation also helps one understand another of the play's most salient features. The audience is constantly reminded that Theopropides has at his disposal whips, crosses, and all the machinery for meting out authoritarian punishment. Although he never gets to use this machinery (by the rules of comedy, it would be unthinkable for him to do so), this steady barrage of allusions has the effect of adding an element of tension and menace to the situation and of reminding the audience of serious and consequential issues lurking in the background. Such allusions raise two questions. Why is the issue belabored in such a programmatic way? Also, these threats serve to remind us of the armory of punishment and repressive violence available to a truly authoritarian father. And yet at the same time they establish a problematic contrast between the figure of such a terrifying father and the weak simpleton who actually embodies fatherhood in the play. Why did Plautus adopt this strategy?

The answers to these questions cannot be fully answered until we turn to a second way of reading *Mostellaria*, which employs social rather than psychological insights. Nevertheless, according to a psychological reading we can understand at least one component of Plautus' intentions in loading this play with so many allusions to the condign punishment of slaves. If Tranio is a kind of son-surrogate embodying the Oedipal son's dynamism and aggression, then surely such threatened violence equally represents the Oedipal son's guilt-induced dread of paternal retribution. Having these punishments hang over Tranio has the effect of shifting the anxiety as well as the guilt away from the son-figure in the play: it is notable that Theopropides, who has every reason in the world to be irate at Philolaches, never issues any especially dire threats against him. The audience is invited to laugh at these threats in their transmuted and comical guise: comical because the audience knows full well that they will not be put into effect, and because they hang over a character toward whom the spectator is invited to adopt an attitude of superiority.

Theopropides is not characterized as especially austere or as pathologically authoritarian, and so is not a figure of great menace. Rather, his salient qualities are stupidity, gullibility, silly superstition, and weakness, and throughout the play he is humiliated and reduced to a figure of fun as his powerlessness is revealed to the spectator. The object here is obviously to deflate the prestige of fatherhood. It may not be entirely amiss to suggest that, just as the more dynamic aspects of the Oedipal son's personality are shifted onto Tranio, so some of the Oedipal father's grim and austere characteristics are transferred to the slave Grumio. What is left is a silly, impotent old man.

Seen from one point of view, Simo is another of those young-at-heart old men who remain fun-loving and in touch with the values of Dionysus. But viewed from another angle he is a kind of surrogate figure onto whom have been shifted the attractive features that a father like Theopropides should but does not have. He is an elder man who is tolerant, nonthreatening, and who poses no obstacles to the son and therefore elicits no feelings of guilt. Like Micio in Terence's *Adelphoe*, he therefore stands as a kind of son's fantasy figure of what an ideal father might be like and how he could be perceived, if only the whole burden of the Oedipal situation and its attendant feelings of hostility and guilt could be dispensed with.

The analysis of comedy, no less than any other kind of literature, requires some sort of theoretical underpinning. It also requires some sort of agreed-upon discourse. If Aristotle did write a Book II of the *Poetics*, he evidently made catharsis the centerpiece of his discussion of comedy as well as of tragedy. It is easy to see the attraction of this strategy; it is in fact easier than in the case of tragedy insofar as comic psychic catharsis can be correlated with a distinctly cathartic physiological event, laughter. Over the past couple of decades in particular, the idea of the cathartic value of comedy has begun to resurface in critical discussions of ancient comedy, as modern students become increasingly aware of the necessity of some theoretical foundation for their discussions (although one must admit that there exists a wide spectrum of opinions as to what comic catharsis actually is and how it may work).[13]

The idea that the primary function of ancient comedy was to purge the spectator of Oedipal tensions and feelings of guilt, which might be suggested by some of Sigmund Freud's observations on the subject of humor, would be intolerably and absurdly reductionist. But it seems both possible and attractive to argue that such was one kind of catharsis that ancient comedy could provide on occasion. In plays such as *Mostellaria* the Oedipal situation is invoked in more or less disguised, but nevertheless penetrable, forms and its associated hostilities are ventilated. The situation is presented as seen through the son's eyes, so that the son and his allies are represented favorably and the father and his supporters are not. The father is bamboozled, defeated, subjected to various outrages, if not by his son, then at least by the son's allies and surrogates. And so the father (although he is not killed, as some characters have wished) is ultimately shown to be impotent. Divestiture and demystification of paternal power and prestige amount to a kind of symbolic castration. In result, the son achieves his erotic aims. Nonetheless, despite the dark elements provided by the potential violence of paternal authority and the symbolic fulfillment of the wish for the father's death, part and parcel of the plot is a final reconciliation that serves to defuse the situation and eliminate the feelings of guilt and anxiety it has evoked. For, by the invariable rules of the game, the world of comedy is a safe one. This is both because its characters are people to whom the audience is invited to feel superior, and because all of the dangers, threats, and menaces in comedy's world are understood to be spurious and unthreatening.

The insight that both Tranio and Callidamates embody displaced fragments of the Oedipal son's personality serves to render the absence of the son at the play's conclusion comprehensible. The reconciliation between Tranio, Callidamates, and Theopropides, rather than between father and son, has already been discussed. Then too, Plautus helps along the psychological effect of the reconciliation scene by supplying an extra anxiety-reducing detail. At 1149ff. Tranio jeers at Theopropides: "If you are a friend of Diphilus or Philemon, tell them how your slave played a practical joke on you. You would provide them with an excellent example of a baffled man for their comedies." This metadramatic touch, which occurs at an emotionally critical moment, serves to remind the spectator that what he is witnessing is, after all, just a play that need not be taken overseriously.

So, on the psychological level, plays like *Mostellaria* work by evoking Oedipal feelings in the spectator and then purging him of them. But it is doubtful that Freudian analysis by itself tells the whole story, or that *Mostellaria* could be adequately understood by interpreting it as displaced projections of a psychic melodrama. The trouble is that if you adhere rigidly to the Freudian program and place an exclusively Oedipal interpretation on father-son confrontations in Roman comedy, this reading has the effect of pushing off such conflicts into the abstract realm of "the eternal human condition" and thereby depriving them of any sense of immediacy.

For generational conflict is part of the fabric of life. The young envy the power, prestige, and efficacy possessed by their elders, nurturing hopes and dreams of inheriting all of this themselves (presumably not unmixed with complex feelings of aggression and guilt). For them to achieve their personal, economic, social, and professional ambitions, sooner or later their elders must be thrust aside. Or at the very least a "place in the sun" must eventually be negotiated for a younger generation, which involves an element of compromise and yielding on the part of society's seniors. In any male-dominated society, this amounts to a formula for competition and conflict between young men and old men. Within the family context, this means competition and conflict between sons and fathers. The would-be parricide in *The Birds* may be taken as emblematic of this fact. There is nothing visibly Oedipal about him. His stated ambition is purely and simply to inherit his father's property, and there is no reason for doubting his word. With prizes such as prestige, power, and property at stake, the competition for the mother begins to look not so much like an all-powerful, all-determining inner psychic melodrama, but rather (as I have already suggested) like a metaphor for a concrete social reality.

Despite its fictive Greek setting, the actual Romanness of the situation in *Mostellaria* is shown by a number of touches introduced by the author. Thus, for instance, we are thrice told that characters in the play "live like a bunch of Greeks" (22, 64, 960). Tranio speaks of convening a senate in his heart, and also of convening a senate of slaves (688, 1049f.). Simo announces his intention of going to the Forum to dodge his wife (708f.). But the most significant such detail has to do with the punishments threatened to be applied to Tranio. In the absence of any evidence about the Greek prototype of this play, we cannot be sure whether this whole element of slave punishment was at least partially present in Philemon's *Phasma* or whether it has been entirely contributed by Plautus. But we can be sure that, if this element was at all present in his Greek model, Plautus significantly changed and Romanized it. Throughout the play crucifixion is pressed into service as a symbol of the punitive authority of the *paterfamilias*, and crucifixion is of course a distinctively Roman means of punishment. Taken in combination, these considerations suggest a specifically Roman reading of the play. Even though *Mostellaria* has a putatively Greek setting, they are Plautus' means of inviting us to view the play's events as if they were occurring in a Roman social context.

If we are to read the play in this manner, its events acquire a specific and somewhat different meaning. Viewed in this light, *Mostellaria* tells the story of a rebellion within the *familia*. Philolaches may be a free son and Tranio a slave but, each in his own way, both are supposed to be bound by *familia* discipline and to display upward-directed obedience and loyalty toward the *paterfamilias*. Besides ignoring his duty of *pietas*, Philolaches is guilty of a second serious infraction of *familia* discipline. He squanders family property for his own dubious purposes, thereby placing his own interests ahead of the collective welfare of the *familia*. On the other hand, he does not commit a second possible breach of *pietas*. Roman sons were supposed to submit to arranged marriages contracted for the advancement of the *familia*, and inappropriate self-chosen love matches were out of the question. In *Mostellaria* it is never said that Philolaches' ambition is to marry his girlfriend. But in other plays similarly disloyal sons indeed are guilty of this form of disloyalty, although a frequent part of inevitable final reconciliations is that such girlfriends are ultimately discovered to be not as inappropriate choices as they first seem.

Ostensibly Philolaches, always egged on by Tranio, is rebelling against the constraints of *pietas* out of sheer hedonism, and from this limited standpoint Mommsen's harsh judgement of comic values is not entirely unjustified. But on a deeper level, Philolaches' real malfeasance is that he is flying the Jolly Roger of individualism. He has placed his own values and interests ahead of the welfare of the *familia,* and in this sense it scarcely matters exactly what these values and interests are.

According to a Roman interpretation, the comic handling of Theopropides also acquires a different significance. A large part of the play's purpose is to lampoon a *paterfamilias*. Various tactics are adopted to achieve this. When Theopropides is shown to be stupid, gullible, superstitious, and wholly ineffectual, his essential weakness is revealed. Even a lowly slave can outthink him and is a more dynamic and creative human being than himself. There is thus a striking contrast between what a *paterfamilias* is supposed to be and what this father actually is. Furthermore, the steady barrage of references to the machinery of torture, whipping, and crucifixion at the disposal of the *paterfamilias* for the purpose of enforcing *familia* discipline can now be seen to play a significant function. They serve as a sort of baseline whereby we can measure the disparity between the powers theoretically vested in Theopropides and his actual weakness, making the latter appear all the more thoroughgoing.

This is especially so because, on this level, the play does not conclude on any real note of reconciliation. To be sure, *Mostellaria* has a plot resolution sufficient to satisfy the needs of comedy and a reconciliation that is adequate for an emotionally satisfying conclusion. But from the present viewpoint it is striking and significant that the play features a reconciliation between Theo-propides, Tranio, and Callidamates, but nothing of the kind between Theopropides and Philolaches. There are no grounds for thinking that a repentant son will mend his ways, abandon his expensive habits, and resume the proper discipline of *pietas* toward his father. And we are given plenty of reason for suspecting that Tranio will continue on his roguish career. And so the play does not end with any kind of recuperation of Theoprop-ides' paternal authority or restoration of *familia* discipline. Rather, the concluding impression is that the erstwhile wholeness of the *familia* has been ruptured permanently—and that this is no bad—or fatal—thing. In this sense, the only genuine reconciliation at the play's conclusion is that Theopropides is obliged to reconcile himself to a changed state of affairs within his household. The success of the rebellion is acknowledged. We shall see similar endings in the other Plautine comedies examined in this study, which conclude with a gesture of paternal surrender.

Mostellaria is another play in which the characters fall into two distinct and readily identifiable camps. On one side are the fun-lovers (Philolaches, which is what the name means in Greek, Tranio, Callidamates, with Simo as an ally) and on the other the *paterfamilias* Theopropides and his gloomily harsh slave Grumio, to whom can probably be added the badgering moneylender Misargyrides, since he is a representative of the workaday world and its responsibilities. True to the logic of comedy, the members of the former camp are portrayed as attractive human beings, while those on the agelastic side are represented unsympathetically. This of course helps orient the spectator's feelings: everything about the play invites the audience to sympathize with and cheer for the rebels against *pietas* and to hope for the defeat of the characters ranged against them.

In view of all that has been said, it is obvious that one of *Mostellaria*'s major functions is to exert some sort of cathartic function vis-à-vis the figure of the *paterfamilias*, over and above any kind of cathartic value it may have in connection with the spectator's Oedipal guilts and anxieties. The idea of the play is not just to expose Theopropides as a weak and ineffectual father, but in so doing to mount an attack on the very idea of authoritarian fatherhood.

As intimated earlier, a major function of comic catharsis is a debunking one. The comic poet takes a look at some individual or institution that has the power to intimidate the spectator in real life. More precisely, he establishes a stage-surrogate for that person or institution. Then, by a series of techniques he strips this surrogate of its aura of prestige. Such techniques include exposing the surrogate's actual weakness and consequent hypocrisy and portraying it in a grotesque and unflattering light. The surrogate is thus held up to public humiliation. The spectator is invited to laugh at this surrogate, and the laughter has the value of purging him of some of the awe and intimidation that the surrogate's real-life equivalent inspires, and also invites him to adopt an attitude of superiority to and dislike for the surrogate. The ultimate idea is that something of these attitudes will rub off on the spectator toward the person or thing represented by the surrogate, and that person or thing's prestige and capacity to intimidate will be impaired. Thus comedy has the power to instruct the spectator's feelings toward people and things in the real world.

This kind of comic mechanism can be seen at work in any editorial-page cartoon, and this is the psychological mechanism at work in his plays when Aristophanes lampoons pretentious people and institutions and particularly when he lambastes his enemies. So by invoking the cathartic–deflative machinery of comic ridicule, Plautus is trying to instruct the feelings of the spectator no less than did Aristophanes.

This is why the suggestion deserves to be made that *Mostellaria* be read as a contemporary Roman sociopolitical document. *Mostellaria* does two things that are highly subversive of the *mos maiorum*. It mounts a comic attack on the figure of the *paterfamilias* and at the same time it suggests an alternative to *pietas*, insinuating that junior members of the *familia* have lives of their own, have their own ambitions to fulfill, and deserve the freedom to pursue them. It also suggests that slaves are interesting and worthwhile human beings in their own right (in some of his other plays Plautus makes the same point about women).

Mostellaria is scarcely an isolated example. A number of other Plautine comedies also seem calculated to undermine the austere and forbidding image of the *paterfamilias* (just as others appear meant to undermine Catonistic values in other ways—a couple of these will be noted at the end of this chapter). Some of these more or less resemble *Mostellaria* in that practical jokes are played on a father so that a son may enjoy a ladylove. In several of these, the trickery is achieved by a clever slave of the Tranio type. Such plays are *Bacchides*, *Epidicus*, *Pseudolus*, and *Trinummus*. Three Plautine comedies (*Asinaria*, *Casina*, and *Mercator*) are variants of a different type of father–son conflict, in which father and son are competing for the same sexual object. We may now turn to this latter type of play, as represented by *Asinaria* and *Casina*.

Asinaria

We are informed by its prologue that *Asinaria* ("The Comedy of Asses") is based on the play *Onagos* (The donkey) by the New Comedy poet Demophilus. The play begins with a conversation between a gentleman named Demaenetus and his slave Libanus. It is unusual because, for all the difference between their social stations, they are trading good-natured insults as if they were equals. But it soon becomes apparent that Demaenetus has a problem, and he is trying to enlist Libanus' aid.

Demaenetus knows full well that his son Argyrippus is infatuated with the courtesan living next door. Her name is Philaenium, and she is currently spurning him because he has run out of money. Far from being upset with his son for this escapade, Demaenetus sympathizes with him. Indeed, his intention is to supply him with the necessary money to continue the affair.

This is a remarkable attitude for a comic father. But Demaenetus explains his reasoning:

> Libanus, all parents who listen to me will be a bit flexible in dealing with their children. Thus they will find their sons more loving and well disposed. And I want to act thus, I want to be loved by my kinsmen. I want to imitate my own father. For my sake he dressed himself up as a sea captain and played a trick to get the girl I loved out of the hands of a pimp. He felt no shame in playing up to me and purchasing his son's love. And I've made up my mind to imitate his policy. For today Argyrippus my son said that he was in love and asked me for some money, and I very much want to oblige the boy. His mother keeps him under strict control, the way fathers normally do. But I say to hell with all that. Especially because he thought me worthy to receive his confidences, I am obliged to respect his nature. Since he has come to me, as a dutiful son should, I want him to have some money for his girlfriend. (64ff.)

Libanus sympathizes, but points out the difficulty. The obstacle is Demaenetus' wife (we later learn that her name is Artemona): "I know that you are wishing your wish in vain. Your wife has brought along that slave woman Saurea as part of her dowry, and she has more control of the household than you do" (84f.). Demaenetus is obliged to agree: "I took the dowry-money, and in exchange for it I sold off my authority" (86).

This being the case, Demaenetus cannot simply hand over the money to his son. Therefore he invites Libanus to swindle it from him. He does not fully spell out his logic. The evident implication is that he does not have full control over the family exchequer and cannot give the money to his son without Artemona finding out. Therefore he must be able to give her some plausible excuse for its disappearance.

After Libanus' departure Demaenetus explains to the audience that he knows of no slave who is baser or cleverer than Libanus, and so trusts him to make a good job of his commission: certainly he will, since he knows that the alternative is a good thrashing.

The next scene begins abruptly as Argyrippus is forcibly thrown out of the house next door. Since he has run out of money, Philaenium's procuress-mother Cleareta has had him ejected. He stands in front of the house, furiously railing. He is going to report her to the authorities, ruin her and drive her into abject poverty. In the course of this speech he lets slip an interesting fact about himself, one that will receive confirmation later in the play. This is when he refers to her stripping him of all the money he has earned at sea (135). This and a further mention at 599f. about his work as a legislator seem to suggest that he is somewhat more advanced in life and self-sufficient than the average comic *adulescens*.

In response to his outdoor haranguing, Cleareta comes out of the house and rebukes him. She reveals herself as a perfect specimen of her type. She is frankly and cheerfully mercenary and makes no bones about the fact that money is her sole interest. She is impervious to Argyrippus' protests. The matter must rest where it stands: no money, no more Philaenium.

Act II is entirely devoted to the scheme Libanus devises for the mock-swindling of Demaenetus. It seems that Saurea, Artemona's lieutenant, functions as steward of the household (this, no doubt, is why Demaenetus cannot spend his own money with impunity). She has recently sold off some asses. The purchaser is coming with the payment money and, by one of those happy comic coincidences, the sum involved is just the amount demanded by Cleareta. Therefore Libanus hatches his scheme. Another female slave in the household, Leonida, will pretend to be the steward of the household and accept the payment for the asses. But when the purchaser shows up, he creates a difficulty by refusing to give it to anyone but Demaenetus himself.

Act III begins with a short interview between Philaenium and her mother. Philaenium genuinely does love Argyrippus and is heartbroken that her mother is coming between them. Neverthe-less, she cannot make any impression on the mercenary Cleareta and is forced to obey. Then Libanus and Leonida return from the forum and tell the audience how the swindle has proved success-ful. Demaenetus pretended that Leonida was Saurea, and the dealer duly handed over the money for the asses. The third scene of Act III consists of an almost mock-tragic passage between Argyrippus and Philaenium, in which they profess their anguish at parting and their mutual love. They go so far as to enter into a suicide pact. But their love duet is repeatedly punctuated by Libanus and Leonida's clownish interjections.

In the course of this scene Argyrippus reveals to Libanus that the real problem is that a young fellow named Diabolus has promised to pay Cleareta twenty minae for her daughter. Oh, if he only had so much money himself! Libanus urges him to cheer up. It just so happens that he has a wallet containing twenty minae, which he will give Argyrippus if Philaenium will give him a kiss. After a bit of horseplay in which the kiss is duly given and Argyrippus is made to carry Libanus on his back, the sum is handed over.

But the kiss exchanged for the money foreshadows a more serious demand. At the end of the scene, Libanus informs Argyrippus that the money really comes from Demaenetus—but with a condition attached to it. Demaenetus expects his son to provide him not only with a dinner but with Philaenium's sexual services for one night. The boy receives this news with remark-able good cheer. Possibly he is so thrilled to get the twenty minae that the implications of this demand have not sunk in.

Act IV begins with the entrance of Diabolus, the gentleman who wishes to purchase Philaenium from Cleareta. He is accom-panied by his henchman Parasitus. They are anticipating the purchase of the girl's services for an entire year and going over the details of a contract. This depressingly lengthy document is full of clauses restricting Philaenium's freedom and having the overall effect of depriving her of her personhood and reducing her to the status of a thing. They go into Cleareta's house but come right back out, with Diabolus in a state of high fury. He has learnt that he has been forestalled by Demaenetus and has found out about Demaenetus' stipulation that he is to get one night with the girl. Somehow he has even discovered that the money employed by Demaenetus has been swindled from his wife. But he has a plan for getting even. He will tell the whole story to Artemona. Parasitus forestalls him. It would be more becoming if he were to bring the news to her. Diabolus agrees, urging Parasitus to do his worst, and thus the act concludes.

Act V begins with a banquet scene held in Cleareta's house, but the banquet is a very peculiar one. This is the feast Demaenetus has demanded as part of his repayment. We find him ensconced on a couch with Philaenium. Argyrippus is doleful (830ff.):

DEM. My boy, don't you find it disturbing to see her stretched out by me?

ARG. Father, my *pietas* keeps the sight from being painful. Although I love her, I am able to control my mind so that I don't mind it that she's lying with you.

And again (840ff.):

ARG. Hey, look at me. I'm laughing.

DEM. I wish my ill-wishers would laugh like that.

ARG. Father, I know why you think I'm in the dumps, because she's with you now. And to tell you the truth, father, this situation does make me gloomy. But not because I don't wish you to have your way. I really love you. I just wish it were some other girl.

DEM. But I want *this* one.

ARG. So you're getting your wish. I wish I could do the same.

When Demaenetus points out that it is only reasonable to grant him a day's worth of a girl, since he has purchased a year's worth for his son, Argyrippus can only acknowledge (848) that "you've got me hogtied with that deed of yours." These exchanges set the dismal tone for the banquet and show the reasoning behind Argyrippus' gloomy complaisance.

But before the banquet can drag on to its apparently inevitable conclusion, an irate Artemona comes out of Demaenetus' house, accompanied by Parasitus. Parasitus has told her the whole story and she is irate. She thought him to be prudent and self-controlled, a loving husband. But now she discovers that he is a decrepit old whoremonger. He has fobbed her off with lies about dining out with his friends, being at the Senate, assisting his clients, but in fact he has been hanging about brothels, corrupting his son, "plowing other people's farms while leaving his own unplowed" (874). Parasitus invites her to peek in the door and see the truth for herself. She sees Demaenetus, who is growing increasingly amorous. He is promising to steal Artemona's cloak and give it to her. She comments that she has been wondering where all her possessions have been going—she had wrongly been suspecting her servants (888). This detail is interesting, as it suggests that this is not the first time Demaenetus has gone astray.

As Artemona continues to eavesdrop, Demaenetus just manages to make the situation worse. When he asks Philaenium for a kiss, she asks in return why he doesn't kiss his own wife. Does she suffer from halitosis? Probably nodding vigorously, he avers he'd rather drink bilge water. At 901f. and again at 905 he voices wishes for her death. Parasitus is highly pleased, and decides it is time to retire. As he departs he expresses the hope that Diabolus and Argyrippus can agree on some time-sharing arrangement concerning Philaenium. Otherwise he'll probably be done out of a patron. The play then rushes to its inevitable close as Artemona bursts in and catches Demaenetus red-handed. She misunderstands Argyrippus' motive in being there and gives him a good tongue-lashing too. Then the play concludes as Artemona and Philaenium join in mocking Demaenetus.

When we first meet him, Demaenetus seems like an extremely appetizing comic father, the sort of father any son would dream of having. He is easygoing, democratically civil toward the household slaves, and understanding and affably tolerant of Argyrippus' adolescent fun-seeking. His professed motive in asking Libanus to round up sufficient money to purchase Philaenium is that this is his strategy for procuring Argyrippus' love. According to even the harshest moral judgement, such a motive can be regarded as no more than misguided, and certainly is quite understandable. Demaenetus seems to be a father who is keenly aware of the necessity of binding his son to him by ties of affection and mutual trust rather than by harsh parental authoritarianism, and so when we meet him he looks not at all unlike Micio in Terence's *Adelphoe*.

His initial description of the family situation in his speech at 60ff. suggests that we are going to be treated to an inversion of the usual comic situation. In this household, it seems, the normal structure of family authority has been reversed. In Demaenetus' household it is Artemona who is strict and repressive: she has usurped the role normally played by fathers. This has the interesting effect of liberating Demaenetus, who obviously resents her power, from his responsibility, and leaving him free to adopt a policy of liberalism. He therefore seems sympathetic to the normal comic program of freedom and fun, and his negative attitude toward Artemona is comically pardonable insofar as she has assumed the function of fun-spoiler. All of these considerations combine to make us like Demaenetus enormously. As Libanus points out in the first scene, this reversal of roles has the effect of casting Artemona in the role of the agelastic obstacle to the fulfillment of adolescent love. So our initial impression is that we are going to see a play that generates humor in a manner rather like that of Aristophanes' *The Wasps*, by presenting a comically inverted parody of normal power relationships within a family.

Therefore the spectator is misled by Demaenetus' initial representation of the facts, no less than is Argyrippus. In his speech at 60ff. Demaenetus recalls that in his youth he was party to a similar romantic escapade. So, in effect, he acknowledges that he is no different and no better than his son, and in the sequel we learn that he means what he says—with a vengeance. Possibly his insistence on spending a night with Philaenium is no more than a sudden deplorable whim. But the insinuation at 888 that he has a past history of similar behavior suggests a more sinister implication: slaking his lust on Philaenium has been his goal all along. If so, all his initial talk about liberality and concern for winning his son's affection is nothing but a monstrous piece of hypocrisy. And since Argyrippus, tricked into believing his spurious posturings, has confided his problems to him, Demaenetus also stands guilty of having abused his son's confidence.

The most remarkable feature of the play is the dejected passivity with which Argyrippus defers to his father in this matter.

Asinaria presents us with characters capable of deeper feelings than those who populate *Mostellaria*. The love between Argyrippus and Philaenium is real and reciprocal. Argyrippus' passivity in the face of Demaenetus' appropriation of his girlfriend forms a striking contrast to the assertive indignation with which he has railed against Cleareta in Act I. This initial scene certainly shows that he is no milksop by nature and that, when he feels he is being abused, he is capable of lodging a sharp protest and threatening dire retribution. Likewise, in his scene with Philaenium he demonstrates a considerable capacity to register emotion. So why not now? Surely the reasons he himself gives in Act V strike us as unconvincing in view of the unreasonableness of Demaenetus' demands.

From a psychological point of view, the reason for Argyrippus' apathy is not hard to ascertain. By its very nature, the essential plot situation, which casts a father and a son as rivals for a single woman, invokes the Oedipal situation. If you want to think that the purpose of this comedy is to arouse the spectator's Oedipal anxieties and hostilities so that they can be purged by comic laughter, then the initial situation is by itself sufficiently evocative to accomplish this goal. Showing the spectator any kind of actual hostile confrontation between father and son would probably go too far in this direction and arouse stronger feelings than comic catharsis could handle. Therefore such a confrontation must be avoided. (This is why Plautine sons such as Philolaches may express sentiments of hostility toward their fathers behind their backs or in asides, but not to their faces.)

So Plautus adopts a strategy not entirely unlike that employed in *Mostellaria*. Just at the point in the play where Argyrippus should react with shock, outrage, and anger, and ought to take steps to defeat his father's aggression, Diabolus and Parasitus just happen to pop up. Although for a very different ostensible reason, Diabolus displays very much the same range of emotions that Argyrippus ought to exhibit, but does not. Likewise, while Argyrippus remains virtually paralyzed with apathy, Diabolus takes bold countermeasures that prove successful and bring about Demaenetus' downfall.

None of this is coincidental. On a psychological level, Diabolus and his lieutenant Parasitus are functioning as surrogates for Argyrippus. Both his emotional reactions and his aggression are shifted over onto these characters, which is why he himself is devoid of them. Thus they can express the feelings, and carry out the aggressive action, of the Oedipal son without provoking the same emotional response in the spectator that would occur if Argyrippus himself were to react in the expected way. This argument is particularly attractive because of their names. Any spectator with a smattering of Greek would appreciate that Diabolus and Parasitus are not personal names at all, but merely words that specify the functions they perform in the play: "Denouncer" and "Hanger-On." Their names reveal an important inner truth about them: they are not normal characters, endowed with individual names and personalities. Their names tell us that they are merely personified functions. They are, in other words, mere straw men hustled in to perform their necessary surrogate duties.

The play of course invites the spectator to observe the contrast between what fathers are and what fathers ought to be. At the beginning of the play Demaenetus frankly avers that he is no better than his son, and his father no better than he. Did his father exploit him as cynically as he exploits Argyrippus? Will Argyrippus abuse his own son in turn? At the very least, there is something very hypocritical about Demaenetus, and this speech has a possible generalizing effect. Are fathers always hypocritical? Are fathers never any wiser or better than adolescent mooncalf sons?

The circumstantial facts supplied by Demaenetus may even suggest a more concrete possibility. When he talks about his father (his name was Strato—cf. 344) disguising himself as a shipmaster to swindle a slave dealer into giving him a girl he himself loved, this sounds remarkably like the premise of a New or Roman comedy. Maybe this is an allusion to some specific play, possibly one for which Demophilus' *Onagros* was conceived as a sequel. In any event, this touch gives one an odd view of life, that it is a series of comic plots strung together, so that each generation repeats the experience of its predecessor without acquiring any visible wisdom in the process, and so that a given man will first be cast in the role of a comic son, and then in that of a comic father.

In *Asinaria* the attack on the prestige of fatherhood works differently than that of *Mostellaria*, because although Theopropides is a gullible bumbler, he is not hypocritical. Or rather, he is only hypocritical in the general sense that there is a considerable disparity between what he is and what fathers are advertised to be. Nor is Theopropides selfish, and he does not exploit his paternal role for deplorable purposes. But despite the different strategies adopted, the net effect remains the same: the demystification of the father figure and even, if you insist, his symbolic castration. In *Asinaria* this is achieved by revealing the hypocrisy of Demaenetus' motives, and also by subjecting him to a humiliating reversal at the hands of his dread wife. So, each in its own way, both plays induce the spectator to ask the same questions. Is this a really powerful father that must be obeyed and needs to be feared? Is this a father to be taken seriously? The spectator might find it exhilarating and liberating to discover that fatherhood's pretensions are bogus.

Like *Mostellaria*, *Asinaria* is not without Romanizing touches that invite the spectator to look at Demaenetus as if he were a Roman *paterfamilias*. Argyrippus avows that he is granting his father access to Philaenium out of a sense of *pietas* (831). If Roman sons are supposed to exhibit dutiful *pietas* toward their fathers, are fathers permitted to abuse their dutifulness so cynically? Is *pietas* then simply a device that permits fathers to dupe their sons? In this context it is worth pointing out that *pietas* is a very specific Roman word denoting a very specific Roman concept. There is no equivalent word or concept in Greek, and so the use of *pietas* at this critical juncture in the play must be accounted a tellingly deliberate Romanizing touch. Likewise, Artemona talks about his stories that he is busy in the Senate or helping his clients (871), and the patron–client relationship was a Roman cultural institution equally foreign to the Greeks.

With the exception of the expressions of love voiced by Argyrippus and Philaenium, the tone of the play operates only on the level of somewhat cynical lightheartedness. Save for Diabolus' reaction, rationalized as that of a man who merely feels that he has been cheated on a business transaction, Demaenetus' sexual aggressiveness stirs up no serious feelings of repulsion or outrage. The portrayal of the pain his action causes the lovers is very muted, in comparison to the way their anguish is aroused by the prospect of being separated at Cleareta's decree. Artemona's reaction is one of anger and exasperation. She grimly rolls up her sleeves to inflict richly deserved punishment on her wandering husband. But, to invoke that long-gone comic strip once again, the kind of punishment involved is not unlike that Maggie used to visit on Jiggs. In her case too, there is no portrayal of genuine pain or spiritual anguish.

If anything, the play reflects a bit of the easy cynicism exhibited by a number of its characters. Demaenetus has no compunctions about abusing his son's confidence, love, and sense of *pietas* in order to achieve a sleazy sexual triumph. Cleareta is a hardened procuress with her eye fixed firmly on the obol. Diabolus regards possession of Philaenium as a simple business deal, and Parasitus, true to his name, seems interested only in advancing his own cause and getting a bit of amusement in the bargain. Young love stands only a slender chance of success in a world like this. Are Argyrippus and Philaenium fated to grow up and become people like their parents?

When the story is told in this way, with no real pain shown, the spectator is free to respond with detached amusement. But, obviously, it would be possible to tell the same story in considerably different terms, where a father's sexual rivalry with his son causes real pain and where a genuine element of moral outrage is present. In this case, a hypocritically predatory father would look like a true villain and his comeuppance would be portrayed as an act of substantial justice. Couple that with sufficient Romanizing touches to remind the spectator that he is a *paterfamilias*, and you would concoct a much more powerful drama, capable of producing real shock. This is what Plautus accomplished in *Casina*.

Casina

Casina is based on a comedy by Diphilus, another contemporary of Menander, entitled *Cleronomoi* (The lot-drawers). The play is about the situation in the household of a gentleman named Lysidamas, but the details of this situation only become evident to the spectator as the play unfolds (the prologue that prefaces the play was obviously written after the fact by someone else). The first scene is rather similar to that of *Mostellaria*. Two slaves, Olympio and Chalinus, are having a quarrel. Both want to marry a girl named Casina, and each is dead sure of his own impending success. Chalinus ridicules Olympio for his attachment to the countryside and bids him go back to his farm (103). A little later (117ff.), in predicting his success, Olympio promises that Chalinus will be obliged to serve as torchbearer at the wedding—then he will be dragged off to the farm, where an extremely unpleasant future on the slave-gang awaits him, and where he will be nourished by a starvation diet.

At first it looks as if the competition for Casina involves only these two slaves. But in the next scene more of the true situation is revealed. Cleostrata, Lysidamas' wife, comes out. She is beside herself with rage, thundering imprecations against her husband "who sets himself against me and my son to gratify his lustful whim" (149f.). Her good friend Myrrhina, the mistress of the next-door household, joins her and she confides her problem. She has a private maid of her own, with whom Lysidamas has fallen in love, and he has decided to marry her to his farm-bailiff Olympio. More precisely, the verb used to designate Lysidamas' feelings for Casina is *amat*, but it would take us too far afield to inquire what this verb actually means. In Roman comedy, under what circumstances and to what degree does *amor* correspond to the modern experience of romantic love? Here, quite clearly, nothing but sexual infatuation is indicated. Cleostrata is livid and wants to do something about it, but Myrrhina (kind of a comic equivalent of Sophocles' Chysothemis or Ismene) counsels a passive attitude. After all, whatever a wife owns belongs to her husband, and if she holds back any private property she is in effect stealing from him. And Cleostrata must at all costs be afraid of that ultimate husband's formula *ei foras mulier* ("woman, get out of my house"), for by doing no more than saying these words a husband can divorce his wife and throw her into the street.

Lysidamas enters, smug, self-satisfied with his new love, and positively reeking of perfume. He delivers himself of a monologue in which he frankly acknowledges "my wife torments me—by being alive" (227). He is also unkempt, and he has been drinking. Cleostrata meets him and taxes him for his appearance, behavior, and ungodly smell.

They fall into a fight. Lysidamas bluntly asks if she has reconciled herself to letting him have his way. He wants to marry Casina to the bailiff, so that she can lead a decent life, rather than yielding to Cleostrata's plan of marrying her to that worthless shield bearer who hasn't a dime to his name. His wife retorts that he must be forgetting his station in life. Worrying about the maids is the wife's responsibility. We both ought to assist our son by marrying Casina to the orderly.

Lysidamas, presumably because he is in his cups, gives an exceedingly boorish response (263f.): "that boy isn't my only son—any more than I'm his only father." This one line suffices to indicate his character. In the course of their fencing Lysidamas makes a lame joke that will be played upon later, to the effect that he is Jupiter and his wife is Juno (229f.). The point here is that Jupiter was always seducing mortal girls, and was consequently henpecked by his constantly wronged consort. Shortly thereafter they come to an agreement of sorts: each of them will try to persuade the other's pet slave to give up the idea of marrying Casina.

Lysidamas begins, in an interview with Chalinus. He reminds the slave of his position: "first of all, I want you to keep a straight face while talking to me. It's stupid for you to look gloomy when talking to somebody who has more power than you do" (281f.). Having thus established the tone of the conversation with his customary affability, Lysidamas offers Chalinus his freedom if he will give up his claim on Casina, but the slave smoothly retorts that if he were free he would have to live at his own expense rather than being supported by his master. In exasperation, Lysidamas orders that a water-urn be produced so that the slaves can draw lots for the girl. When Chalinus expresses optimism that he will draw the lucky one, Lysidamas snorts that the only thing he will be allotted is a horrible death by crucifixion (300).

So Lysidamas gets nowhere with Chalinus and dismisses him. Olympio arrives, backing out from a conversation with Cleostrata within the house. He too is exasperated and complains to Lysidamas (319f.): "you're like a hunter; you pass your life spending your days and nights—with a dog!" Lysidamas agrees that his wife is a problem (326): "how I wish her belly had burst open," and Olympio retorts "it would have—if you were a good fertilizer." Lysidamas once more calls himself Jupiter, which provokes the cynical retort (333ff.): "All this is great nonsense. As if you aren't aware how quickly these human Jupiters drop dead." Likewise, when Lysidamas says that heaven will direct the lottery in his favor, the slaves points out how often those mortals who trust in heaven are deceived (347ff.).

At Lysidamas' behest, Cleostrata and Chalinus enter to participate in the drawing. Rather bewildered, the wife asks her slave what her husband wants of her, and Chalinus is entirely honest (353): he wishes to see you blazing on your funeral pyre. In a conversation before the lottery begins, Lysidamas makes one final effort of persuasion, but by an unfortunate slip of the tongue he says "I wish, dear wife, that I could prevail on you to let me marry Casina" (364f.). When he is challenged, he hastily stammers that he meant to say "let *him* marry Casina." Trying to placate Cleostrata, he makes a fuss about acknowledging her rights within the household, but achieves nothing.

Meanwhile Olympio keeps up his bluster, threatening evil things for Chalinus, including the rather extravagant promise that he will be obliged to blow his eyeballs out through his nose (391). He even accuses Cleostrata of employing witchcraft to affect the outcome of the lottery (388). When Chalinus speaks up, Lysidamas orders Olympio to smash him in the face, which promptly occurs. At last the drawing takes place, and Olympio wins. He smugly boasts that this has happened because of the *pietas* of himself and his ancestors (418). Lysidamas gruffly bids Cleostrata go inside and do his bidding, as the wedding preparations must now be made.

The stage clears, leaving alone an extremely dejected Chalinus. The thought of suicide crosses his mind, but he decides not to: he should have to submit to the expense of buying a rope, and in any event his death would only please his enemies. While he is in the midst of such gloomy reflections he hears Lysidamas and Olympio approaching and steps back so that he can overhear them. They are gloating over their shared victory and over Chalinus' discomfort. There follows a curious incident (452ff.). Lysidamas is so overwrought by anticipation of consummating his lust for Casina that he demands that Olympio offer him his lips: he tries to make love to the man. The hidden Chalinus is astonished, as the old man seems to be trying to sodomize his slave on the spot (455) and Olympio has to tell him to "get your-self off my back" (459). Chalinus realizes that this is why he has made Olympio his bailiff, and recalls the time that Lysidamas once offered to make him his porter: "this old geezer always did yearn for bearded faces" (466).

After Olympio manages to fend off his master, Lysidamas reveals his clever plan. He has persuaded his next-door neighbor Alcesimus to lend him his house. Cleostrata will invite Alcesi-mus' wife to participate in the wedding, and while everybody thinks Olympio has taken his bride off to the country he himself will be free to enjoy her in Alcesimus' empty home.

Lysidamas and Olympio exit, leaving Chalinus in exultation. Now he knows Lysidamas' shoddy scheme. He can reveal it to his mistress, and then they can turn the tables on the old reprobate.

Toward the beginning of Act III an indignant Cleostrata appears. Chalinus has divulged Lysidamas' secret to her. Her own scheme is to ruin Lysidamas' plan by the simple device of not inviting Alcesimus' wife to the wedding: if she is still at home, Lysidamas can scarcely have his way with Casina. She has some scorn left over for Alcesimus, who she describes sarcastical-ly (and in a very Roman way) as "that pillar of the Senate, that champion of the People" (536). Alcesimus greets her and express-es his puzzlement that she has not invited his wife to help with the wedding preparations. With mock-innocence she replies that no help is needed, and despite his heavy-handed hints Alcesimus cannot induce her to change her mind. He is left behind in frustration, and vents his fury against Lysidamas for having maneuvered him into this awkward position: he is a worthless goat, a toothless old coot (550). Cleostrata, in a mono-logue that immediately follows, reinforces this impression of her husband. He is a decrepit old man (559) and "if you were to see his severe countenance, you'd think that he was austere!" (562).

A frustrated Lysidamas enters. In the typical manner of a Roman upper-class gentleman, he has been obliged to waste a whole day serving as *advocatus* for a relative in some legal matter (567). He bumps into his wife, and with feigned solicitude asks after her welfare. Hasn't she invited Myrrhina over to help her? Cleostrata lies that Alcesimus has had some sort of fight with the woman and refuses to let her out of the house.

Immediately after this interview Lysidamas meets Alcesimus, and reproves him for going back on his promise to get Myrrhina out of the house. The neighbor replies that Cleostrata herself told him that his wife's assistance was unnecessary. Although both of these old men are a bit testy, the misunderstanding is straightened out and Alcesimus goes off to fetch Myrrhina.

But before Lysidamas' plan can be put into motion, a tumult suddenly erupts. Cleostrata's maid Pardalisca comes running out of the house shrieking. In terror she runs up to Lysidamas. Casina has gone berserk within the house. She has taken up a sword and is trying to kill Olympio. In her fury she won't let anybody come near her. Furthermore, since she knows that this wedding is Lysidamas' idea, she has threatened not to let either him or Olympio live through the night. But in the midst of giving this dire news to Lysidamas she turns to the audience and tells it the truth (683ff.): this is all a trick devised by Cleostrata and Myrrhina.

Lysidamas is shaken, but collects himself and tries to reassert his authority (700ff.): "Well, even if she does not wish to, she's going to be married today. Why shouldn't I carry out my plan, that she marry me?" But he immediately corrects himself and says that the idea is that she marry his bailiff, claiming that fear has caused him to misspeak himself. So he hustles Pardalisca into the house with orders that the wedding preparations must continue.

Olympio enters, with a train of attendants bringing food for the wedding. Since he has been newly manumitted by Lysidamas and realizes that his cooperation is necessary for the old man's success, his head is swollen with arrogance. He does not bother hiding his contempt for Lysidamas. When (726) his master remarks on this, his response is "foo, your talk stinks," and a bit later (731) he goes so far as to ask "won't you get away from me, unless you want me to puke?" Lysidamas is forced to swallow these insults and positively grovel (738): "I'm your slave...I implore you, my Olympus, my father, my patron." Using the language of the Roman client–patron relationship, Lysidamas acknowledges this virtual reversal of their normal roles. To such a pass has his lust for Casina brought him.

At the beginning of Act IV Pardalisca reappears to inform the audience of the situation within the house. Olympio is strutting about in his bridegroom's costume. Cleostrata and her confederate Myrrhina are busy dressing up Chalinus as the bride. Meanwhile, Lysidamas is hugely oppressed by hunger, but the cooks are inventing hundreds of reasons why he cannot eat—so that they may have all the food for themselves.

The wedding procession enters, with Pardalisca escorting the "bride." She offers some wise advice for a newlywed (816ff.): "Make a sound beginning of your journey through marriage, so that you will always have the upper hand over your husband, that you will always have the power, conquer your man, and be victorious. Let your proclamations and *imperium* prevail. Let your husband clothe you—and you plunder him. Remember, I pray, to cheat your husband night and day."

The remainder of Act IV is taken up with the wedding ceremony itself, with much humor being extracted from the strange appearance and behavior of the supposed "bride."

Act V deals with the sequel of this hilariously inappropriate mock-wedding. Cleostrata, Myrrhina, and Pardalisca gather outside the bridal chamber to enjoy the fun. Myrrhina gives vent to the metadramatic observation that "no poet ever devised a cleverer trick than this invention of ours" (861f.). Cleostrata gives vent to her hope that "the old man would come here with his face smashed in, since there's never been a more wicked old fellow" (862f.). She orders Pardalisca to stay there on guard, so that Lysidamas might be properly humiliated when the truth is revealed.

The women hide and a crestfallen Olympio appears: "I don't know where to flee, where to hide, or how to conceal this humiliation, so greatly have my master and I disgraced ourselves with our wedding-scheme. Thus I am now ashamed, terrified, and we are both laughingstocks. But I in my folly have done something strange: I am ashamed, I who have never felt shame in my life" (874ff.). He goes on to describe graphically how he took his "bride" to bed, and the shock he felt when he started groping "her" and suddenly discovered he was pawing a man's genitals. He is obliged to confess his total humiliation to the women.

Lysidamas fares no better. His *canticum* at 937ff. is imperfectly preserved, but it is clear that he realizes he is completely defeated and that he has no alternative but to grovel before Cleostrata, begging for her mercy. He acknowledges (950ff.) that he deserves a thrashing no less than if he were a disobedient slave.

Cleostrata, Myrrhina, and Chalinus arrive and jeer at him, thoroughly enjoying his embarrassment. He indeed does grovel before his wife, and the final issue of the play is whether she will or will not grant him pardon. He grants her permission in advance to hang him up and give him a whipping if he ever commits such an act again (1002ff.), and she consents to forgive him, but only "lest we make this play last any longer" (1006), and the action does in fact come to a quick end. The play concludes with a short epilogue: Casina will be found to be a daughter of Alcesimus, and so she can marry Lysidamas' son Euthynicus.

Although Lysidamas and his son are vying for the affections of Casina, the actual competition devolves on their respective agents, Olympio and Chalinus. Since the two slaves are overtly surrogates for Lysidamas and his son, it is especially easy to argue that they function as personifications of the more aggressive aspects of the Oedipal father and son. The same mechanism is at work as in *Mostellaria*: "Unacceptable" behavior, speech, and feelings can be given freer expression by slave-characters toward whom the spectator can hold an attitude of superiority. Lysidamas and the son may be competitors but do not display overt aggression or hostility toward each other, and the son's role in the competition is highly attenuated. These traits are displaced onto Olympio and Chalinus, and the inner meaning of the play's hostility-laden first scene only becomes fully comprehensible in retrospect.

Given the very strikingly Oedipal geometry of its dramatic situation, the remarkable thing about *Casina* is the way that the son himself is thrust into the background. He never appears on the stage, nor does Casina. We are told virtually nothing about either of them; we do not even learn the son's name until the epilogue. What is his attitude toward Casina? Does he love her and want to marry her? How precisely does Casina feel about being placed in her peculiar position?

The reason that such questions are moot is that Chalinus is the son's representative only in the most notional of ways. Chalinus is really acting on behalf of Cleostrata, and the only person in the play who expresses the wish that the son might marry Casina is

Cleostrata herself. We have no idea whether the son shares this hope. Although the Oedipal situation is invoked, the play focuses on the duel of wits between Cleostrata and Lysidamas.

Cleostrata dominates the play. *Casina* is the ultimate prototype of Beaumarchais' *Le Mariage de Figaro,* but there is one major difference between the classical original and the French adaptation: *Casina* lacks a Figaro. That is to say, Figaro is a clever and dynamic servant in the tradition of Plautine "clever slave" roles. He spins the schemes that keep the plot moving. But in *Casina* there is no need for such a figure. Chalinus is only Cleostrata's catspaw, and unlike the Countess of Almaviva, she does her own thinking. She is perfectly capable of looking after her own interests and hatching her own plots. So we are presented with a retelling of the same sort of story found in *Asinaria,* this time viewed from the mother's viewpoint.

The pretense of giving *Figaro* a Spanish setting fooled nobody, and failed to keep Beaumarchais, Da Ponte, and Mozart out of hot water with the censorship authorities. The Greek setting of *Casina* is every bit as flimsy and unconvincing. For if *Figaro* is an assault on the mores of the French aristocracy, *Casina* is an equally unfriendly attack on the daunting figure of the upper-class *paterfamilias.*

Theopropides in *Mostellaria* may be portrayed as stupid and feckless, and Demaenetus in *Asinaria* may be a hypocritical rascal, but there is nothing compellingly repulsive about either of these fathers. But it would be difficult to imagine a more hateful comic villain than Lysidamas. He is given a wide range of repellent traits, none worse than his hypocrisy.

There is much about him calculated to remind one of a *paterfamilias* of the senatorial class. He lives next door to a "pillar of the Senate and champion of the people," and presumably he has the same social status as his neighbor. He acts as an *advocatus* for a relative. He has a misleadingly austere and august appearance. And yet beneath this imposing facade he is a kind of unfunny Philocleon. He has a number of traits (self-absorption, willfulness, randy old-goatishness, a certain propensity for inflicting suffering on others) similar to Philocleon's, but they are represented as repulsive, not as amusing or endearing.

Incidentally, we do not know how accidental this resemblance between Lysidamas and Philocleon may be. Scholarship has not paid much systematic attention to the possibility that New Comedy poets borrowed from or alluded to elements of Aristophanic comedy (and perhaps other earlier dramatic works as well). Certainly they were a well-read lot, as were many in their audiences, so I see no reason why this possibility can be excluded. We shall see similar possible Aristophanic echoes in the case of Terence's *Adelphoe*.

Lysidamas' obsession with gaining sexual control over Casina is portrayed as frankly predatory, and the curt brutality with which he treats Cleostrata and expects her to defer to his whims is remarkable. He is, in short, portrayed as a tyrant within the *familia*. Significantly, he repeatedly compares himself to Jupiter, just as Philocleon boasts that the power of the Attic jurists makes them Zeus' equals. And Lysidamas' behavior provokes the response that tyrannical oppression inevitably invites: revolution. For, with the single exception of Olympio (who scarcely bothers to conceal his actual contempt for his master and takes every possible opportunity to demonstrate his own superiority), Lysidamas' behavior calls forth the rebellion of the subordinate members of the *familia*, the women and the slaves. This is a much more comprehensive rebellion than that of Philolaches and Tranio in *Mostellaria*. Under the leadership of Cleostrata, nearly the entire *familia* turns against him and casts off his authority. In doing so, they subject the father figure and his surrogate to gross humiliation and comically expose both the depths of his hypocrisy and his inner weakness. Once more, the prestigious image of paternal authority is revealed to be a sham.

As in *Mostellaria*, this new state of affairs remains unchanged at the end of the play, and its resolution scarcely involves a restoration of paternal domination. A new state of affairs, amounting to a new social dispensation, is created, and the play's only "reconciliation" consists of Lysidamas' reconciliation to the fact that it will be enforced permanently.

There is nothing about the play's ending calculated to defuse the play's tense situation or reduce whatever anxieties the play may have provoked in the spectator. Its conclusion aims at a quite different psychological reaction: the relief one experiences when one sees justice being done. For (as we have already seen in the case of Strepsiades) comedy knows all about poetic justice, and *Casina* is preeminently a play about a bad man receiving his just deserts. No kind of mitigating reconciliation that would permit Lysidamas to retain any shred of his former authority or dignity is allowed to blur this effect. Lysidamas undergoes no change of heart that would invite the spectator to moderate his harsh opinion. We are simply encouraged to applaud and approve of his downfall, just as we have hoped for it in the course of the play.

Although the epilogue reminds us of his existence, which would otherwise very likely be forgotten, the son is a more or less incidental beneficiary of this revolution. But it is a revolt created by those whom Lysidamas visibly oppresses during the course of the play. In introducing Plautine comedy earlier in this chapter, I remarked that he characteristically takes the side of the underdog, and in a patriarchal society the young, the women, and the slaves, the unempowered members of the familia, are the most conspicuous victims of paternal authority.

In two Aristophanic comedies a clever and dynamic woman engineers a social revolution: Lysistrata in *Lysistrata* and Praxagora in *The Ecclesiazusae*. In both plays both the "evils" of masculine society and the inner weakness of their ostensibly strong social command are comically exposed: in both, part of the joke is that the women prove stronger, cleverer, and more decisive than the men. *Casina* invites comparison with these Aristophanic works, for Cleostrata engineers a revolution that is no less radical within the domestic society of the *familia*. If part of the genius of Aristophanic comedy consists of standing the world of everyday social reality on its head, *familia* society is no less thoroughly inverted in this play.

But this represents much more than an innocent excursion into fantasy, since the kind of world that is thus being inverted bears a distinct and unfriendly resemblance to actual Roman society. Surely part of Casina's purpose is to provoke ruminations about patriarchal domination of women in the real *familia*, which doubtless had its unfair and brutal aspects. So much, for example, is implied by the reminder that a Roman husband could divorce and abandon his wife by the mere pronunciation of a short legal formula. The play's representation of the way women are cowed into submission by this threat perpetually hanging over them must have been entirely realistic. And what in reality prevented husbands from treating wives as savagely as Lysidamas bullies Cleostrata?

The revelation of Lysidamas' hypocrisy (like that of Demaenetus in *Asinaria*) also serves to raise the prospect of the genuine hypocrisy of a *paterfamilias,* by suggesting a gap between the austere and awe-inspiring image and the shabby reality. In a different way, both *Mostellaria* and *Casina* raise questions about the humanity and fairness of another aspect of the *familia,* the institution of slavery.

Mostellaria, in short, presents the traditional *familia* as repressive in that it serves to thwart the fun-seeking of its junior and subservient members. *Casina* goes a good deal farther and portrays the institution of the *familia* as downright loathsome. Its discipline of *pietas* merely serves the selfish interest of the *paterfamilias,* who seems free to exploit his underlings in any manner he chooses. The *familia* is no more than an engine designed to inflict suffering on its members. *Casina* and *Mostellaria,* by very different routes, arrive at the same conclusion: the overthrow of the *paterfamilias* and the dissolution of the traditional *familia* and its repressive *pietas.* This is represented as being a good thing. By the same token, violation of *pietas* is characterized as a sensible and wholesome activity, and certainly it is a rewarded one; in all three of the plays we have examined the only *familia* members who accept the traditional discipline of *pietas* are portrayed as fools, dupes, or churls.

Plautus' attacks on traditional Roman values are not limited to demolition of the figure of the *paterfamilias.* Thus, for example, *Rudens* (The rope) contrasts traditional Roman ritualistic superstition with genuine heartfelt piety toward the gods, and also contrasts strict legalism with *humanitas. Miles Gloriosus* (The braggart soldier) explodes the image of the soldier, a figure of great prestige in a society so oriented toward militarism. In *Amphitryo* he lampoons the gods, not excluding Jupiter, and although such burlesques of the gods were routine fare for the Greeks we have no guarantee that such humor would have seemed so innocuous in Plautus' Rome. The humor of *Amphitryo* is not as irrelevant to the present subject as it might appear, as the machinery of religion was wheeled up to support the ideology of the *mos maiorum.* So showing Jupiter and Mercury as a pair of predatory and manipulatory rascals, no better than the characters in a comedy, may well have had a certain subversive effect.

Plautine comedies can only be regarded as innocuous if their fiction of thoroughgoing Greekness, with no actual or possible applicability to Roman society implied, is solemnly believed. Plautus goes very much out of his way to make such belief difficult, and so his comedies very frequently have a distinctly subversive intent. Therefore, both in its antiauthoritarian bent and in terms of the specific comic technique of cathartic derision it deploys against the forces of authority and social respectability, Plautine comedy invites comparison with its Aristophanic predecessor.

Chapter 4

Terence

The Nature of Terence's Art

Terence is a comic poet rather neglected in our times. The amount of criticism and scholarship devoted to him is not especially great or penetrating. Even more symptomatic is the fact much modern criticism regards Plautus and Roman Comedy as nearly synonymous, with Terence shoved firmly into the background on the occasions when he is considered at all. Reasons for this lukewarm attitude are not difficult to discern. Plautus fits in very well indeed with modern ideas of what comedy is and ought to be, but Terence does not. His plays are not especially funny, and they are certainly not uproariously joyous and life-affirming. Nor are they pugnaciously antinomian in the manner of Aristophanes and Plautus. There is nothing hilariously cathartic about them. Thus they are difficult to accommodate to modern critical theories, or readers' expectations, about the nature of ancient comedy or of comedy in general.

Terence was willing to reproduce the quieter and more thoughtful tone of his Greek New Comedy models. Most of the specific adaptive and Romanizing touches we find in Plautus are missing. To the extent that Plautus borrowed an outlook and specific features from Italian farce-forms, Plautine comedy is firmly anchored in native Roman soil. Terence's plays are unrelentingly Hellenistic.

Plautus' audience was the holidaymaking Roman people gathered in the Forum. Terence also ostensibly wrote for the kind of theatergoers described in the prologues of some of his plays, but in reality he enjoyed the patronage of progressive, enlightened, and thoroughly Hellenized patricians, Scipio Africanus (the conqueror of Carthage) and his circle. He was not so dependent on popular reception of his work, and he had good reason to concentrate more on catering to the tastes of his patrons. Insofar as he wrote for their consumption, in presenting works reflecting Hellenistic values he was therefore in the position of a man preaching to the converted, and his plays are shaped to appeal to a sophisticated intellectual elite whose idea of comedy may well have been shaped by firsthand contact with the kind of Greek originals from which Terence was working.

If much in Plautine comedy invites a specifically Freudian interpretation, the same is scarcely true of Terence, particularly as he does not invite the spectator to side with sons in their contentions against their fathers in the same straightforward way. One might be tempted to explain this difference between the two playwrights in terms of their personal psychic dispositions, but such an explanation would probably be both superficial and impertinent. For Plautus the especial interest of the Oedipal situation was that it could be co-opted as a powerful sociopolitical metaphor. Terence was not, and was not obliged to be, so concerned with the conflict of Hellenistic and traditional Roman values, and so had no similar use for the Oedipal metaphor.

Instead, he took a wholly different (and much more sophisticated) tack. In some of his tragedies Euripides employed the trick of placing ordinary characters in traditional heroic situations that are highly stressful, where their consequent behavior can be studied. Naturally, they cannot conduct themselves in heroic ways, and so they act out of their weaknesses and foibles rather than out of their strengths, and their motivations are those of recognizable men and women. Critics both admiring and hostile (beginning with Aristophanes, especially in *The Frogs*) have observed that the veneer of mythology-based tragedy often wears very thin in his plays and that he was groping toward a new kind of realistic melodrama.

Terence adopts the comic equivalent of Euripides' strategy. The world of pure comedy is usually populated with simply conceived and one-dimensional characters. He, on the other hand, places three-dimensional human beings in traditional comic situations, and so his plays may be called "psychological" in a very different sense than those of Plautus. They are concerned with the exploration of realistically depicted character.[1] Pure comedy portrays its characters in blacks and whites. This is why I have repeatedly talked about a comedy's *dramatis personae* being divided into two camps. We find a hero, whose enterprise we cheer, and his friends and supporters ranged against his opponents, whose defeat we hope for and applaud. Each character can readily and unambiguously be assigned to one of these sides. And the hero's ultimate victory is decisive and uncomplicated, with the result that the spectator feels unmixed pleasure and relief at the happy outcome.

There is little room for shades of nuanced gray in this formula, nor is there any tolerance for the message that ostensibly happy resolutions may not be as uncomplicated as they first seem. There is, in short, something eternally cartoonlike about pure comedy's simplistic representations of life, just as there is about its pasteboard characters. Terentian comedy defies this tradition. Here too, his strategy is to reproduce traditional comic situations, but in the more complex and nuanced terms of realistic representation.

It does not matter whether you choose to resent Terentian realism as a betrayal of the proper business of comedy or applaud it as a step in the direction of urbane sophistication. The result in either case is the same: he devised a new kind of drama at Rome featuring a transvaluation of traditional comic values, a dissolution of the barrier between comedy and reality. In this transformed world, characters who are neither wholly admirable or totally ridiculous can act out of complex and sometimes self-contradictory motives. They can change and grow over the course of a play. The meaning of a play's events can be equally complex and ambiguous, no less so than the meaning of the events of real life.

Adelphoe

Terence's very different aims and methods are fully illustrated by *Adelphoe* (140 B.C.—all of Terence's plays were produced between 146 and 140 B.C.). In this play, traditional stock New Comedy characters and situations are readily visible, and the reader will immediately see analogues to elements from plays already studied here. Nevertheless, each of these appears in transmuted form so that they simultaneously strike us as familiar and as startlingly new.

Adelphoe (The brothers) is based on a like-named play by Menander. The premise of the play is that a gentleman named Demea has two sons, Aeschines and Ctesipho. He also has a brother, Micio, who is a childless bachelor. Therefore he has allowed Micio to adopt Aeschines, keeping Ctesipho for himself. As Micio explains in his address to the audience at the beginning of the play, he and Demea have been very different kinds of men since boyhood. Demea has always been frugal and hard-working, and lives in the country. He himself, on the other hand, is an easygoing city dweller who has always devoted himself to a life of ease. He is very devoted to Aeschines, and since his primary concern is that the boy love him in return (49f.) he has brought him up very permissively: "I do not regard it is necessary that he do everything in obedience to my paternal authority" (51f.). Rather, he has encouraged the boy to hide nothing from his father, as his theory is that if a son gets in the habit of lying to his father, he will behave dishonorably toward everyone else: "I believe it is preferable to rear sons with tact and liberality, rather than govern them by intimidation" (58).

But, he tells us, Demea is disturbed by this policy. He rebukes his brother for letting the son carouse, chase women, run up bills. But Micio persists in his theory that:

> [Demea] is unreasonably harsh. In my opinion, he is badly mistaken to think that paternal authority is weightier or more enduring than a father's control based on friendship. This is my feeling and what I have persuaded myself: a man who is only forced to do his duty by impending evil, is only afraid as long as the threat hangs over him. If he thinks he can get away with it, he goes back to his natural-born ways. But he whom you join to yourself out of friendship is eager to repay you and will be the same when he's in your presence and

when he's not. It's a father's job to accustom his son to doing 1
voluntarily rather than out of fear. This is the difference betwe
father and a master, and the man who doesn't know how to dc
must confess that he's incompetent at child rearing. (64ff.)

Demea enters and chides Micio for Aeschines' wild beha
Smugly, he contrasts him with the thrifty and sober Ctesipho
remains down on the farm (94ff.). Micio retorts (98ff.) that th
no crime in the sowing of adolescent wild oats. If Demea w
human being, he'd let Ctesipho do the same. For there's onl
alternative: for the boy to await Demea's hoped-for demis
then behave similarly when he is a man (109f.). He himself
dizes Aeschines' behavior. It's his own money, and Demea l
right to complain about how he chooses to spend it.

Demea reiterates that he is troubled about Aeschines.
maintains each father must stick to the rearing of his ow
for to do otherwise would be to rescind Aeschines' adc
Demea grudgingly agrees, and leaves. His departure crea
abrupt change of attitude in Micio. He confesses to the au
that there is much in what Demea says. He was too pr
confess as much in his presence, but in fact he too is distu
Aeschines' profligate behavior. Recently Aeschines ann
that he was tired of whoring and desired to marry. But
seems, he is up to his old tricks. He himself must go and
what is really happening.

In the next scene Aeschines enters, accompanied b
named Bacchis. He has forcibly taken her away from a
slave-dealer named Sannio, and although this gentleman
them expostulating he refuses to give her back. He is sur
is actually freeborn and has made up his mind to rescue l

He takes her in the house leaving Sannio to fulmina
Micio's slave, manages to calm him down. Then Ctesip
ters, and greets Aeschines in the most friendly and grat
As the scene progresses it is gradually revealed to the
that Bacchis is actually Ctesipho's girlfriend and that /
has rescued her on his brother's behalf. At the end of 1
Ctesipho goes into the house to join her.

In the next scene the plot grows more complex. Mici
next-door neighbor a widow named Sostrata. It seem
daughter Pamphila is about to give birth. Aeschines,
has promised to marry her, but now her slave Geta bu

with high indignation informs her how Aeschines has liberated a slave-girl. Geta of course thinks that the boy has done this for his own benefit and his moral sensibilities are outraged. Although most of his imprecations are directed against Aeschines, he has a choice remark left over for Micio (314): "I'd kill that old man for producing such a rascal!" Sostrata is thrown into despair at this development. The girl's reputation is ruined, she has no dowry, and so she will be destitute. There's only one ray of hope. Aeschines gave her a ring, which she can produce as evidence if he denies his responsibility. Geta is to go tell the whole story to Hegio, a friend of her late husband who has always served as her protector.

The next scene begins with the entrance of a wrathful Demea. He has learned about Aeschines' abduction of the girl and, even worse, has gotten wind of the fact that Ctesipho had a hand in the escapade. Syrus comes along and, although he knows the truth, does not disabuse the old man (392ff.):

> SYR. There's a world of difference between you and Micio
> (and I'm not just saying this because you're here). You're
> nothing but wisdom, he's just a bunch of dreams. Would you
> allow your boy to carry on like this?
>
> DEM. Let him? Wouldn't I smell it out six months before he
> started anything?

Syrus goes on to tell him a cock-and-bull story about how upset Ctesipho became with Aeschines because of the escapade, how he hit him with a steady barrage of moral maxims. Demea hears all this reassuring stuff about his boy with great self-satisfaction.

Demea is about to go off to his farm, where he imagines Ctesipho awaits him, when Hegio comes in. Hegio is understandably upset about Aeschines' supposed abandonment of Pamphila, and taxes Demea about it as the girl's birth-shrieks can be heard offstage. All Demea can do is promise to refer the matter to Micio's attention.

After they leave Ctesipho and Syrus reenter. Ctesipho is disturbed because he is supposed to be at home on the farm but he wants to spend the night with Bacchis. Syrus tells him not to worry. He can invent some lie to explain his absence to Demea, and all he has to do to pacify the old man's anger is feed him

some more lies about what a paragon of virtue Ctesipho is. Shortly thereafter, Ctesipho departs and Demea enters. Syrus is as good as his word. He pretends that Ctesipho has just administered a beating both to himself and to Bacchis because Aeschines' malfeasances had put him into a towering rage. Demea is naturally delighted to hear this and is not too careful about investigating the lies Syrus makes up to explain Ctesipho's absence.

They exit and Micio and Hegio enter. Micio has learned the truth about Aeschines' abduction of Bacchis and pacifies Hegio by relating the actual story. When they leave the stage a highly distraught Aeschines enters. He has gone to Sostrata's house to visit Pamphila and has been rudely turned away because they think he has acquired Bacchis for himself and is in the process of breaking his promises. He is shattered. He wants to tell the women the truth.

As he is summoning the nerve to knock at Sostrata's door Micio arrives. Although he knows the truth, he informs the audience in an aside that he'll have a little fun with Aeschines as a means of repaying him for not confiding in him about the whole situation. So he innocently asks the boy why he is standing at Sostrata's door. He is overjoyed to observe that Aeschines is capable of blushing (643), but to continue his deception he makes up a story that, since her father is dead, Pamphila is about to be married off to her nearest male kin.[2] To be sure, her mother has some make-believe story about the girl having a baby by some unknown man, and so she is opposed to such a marriage. Nevertheless, this appointed husband is right now on his way to Athens in order to claim the girl.

Aeschines is of course upset yet again. He expostulates that this arrangement is downright dishonorable: think how the nameless young father of Pamphila's child will feel when she is taken away from it! Micio replies that no unfairness has been committed: after all, there was no wedding. Aeschines cannot take any more of this, and so he breaks down in tears. This causes Micio to drop his pretenses: he reveals that he knows the whole story. Father and son profess their deep love for each other, and Aeschines admits to feelings of shame over his behavior during this episode.

After this touching interview between father and son, Aeschines exits to prepare for his wedding and Demea enters.

He starts to take Micio to task for Aeschines' behavior: in the past he has merely debauched girls like Bacchis; now he seems to be taking after honest freeborn Athenian girls. Micio receives this news with irritating equanimity. He professes not to be at all disturbed by the impending marriage of Aeschines to Pamphila. No point in getting upset over things you can't change; you just have to reconcile yourself to the throw of the dice.

This response has no calming effect on Demea. What, he asks, will happen to Bacchis? With equal blandness Micio announces that she will remain in the house. This horrifies his brother, who broadly hints at the arrangement's sexual implications (750ff.):

> DEM. I presume that you will arrange things so as to have a singing partner.
>
> MIC. Why not?
>
> DEM. And I suppose you will go a-dancing with these women.
>
> MIC. Fine.
>
> DEM. Fine?
>
> MIC. And you can dance along with us, if the need arises.

And so Micio (who of course knows the truth about Ctesipho and Bacchis) goes on teasing Demea, much as he has already teased Aeschines. Demea gives up in exasperation: the whole household is ruined by its excessive prosperity, and Micio is off his head.

Micio leaves and a drunken Syrus comes out. Demea takes this as further evidence of how Micio has let his household go to rack and ruin. He tries to talk to Syrus, but they are interrupted by another slave calling to Ctesipho within. So Demea learns that his son is not at the farm, but in Micio's house drinking. When Micio appears, he tries to remonstrate, but Micio gives him a lecture (896ff.). Demea can stick to his frugal habits, but his own money is a kind of bonus for the boys to enjoy. There's no need for worry; they can be trusted. He sees in them the qualities one wants. They are wise and intelligent; they display deference, mutual affection, and generosity. Even though they may be sowing their wild oats, they can easily be brought back to probity.

Demea might think that they are spendthrifts, but the great fault of old age is an overconcern with money.

This produces a remarkable change of heart in Demea. As soon as Micio departs, he enters into a long soliloquy, worth quoting in full:

> No man can have a plan for his life so well worked out that reality, age, and experience cannot modify by teaching you. You are ignorant of that you imagine you know, and what at first you hold to be true is disproved by experience. This has now happened to me. For now that my life has nearly run its course I'm abandoning the austere life style I have always followed. Why? By experience I have discovered that nothing is better for a man than tolerance and kindness. The truth of this can easily be ascertained by looking at the situation of me and my brother. He is mild, tranquil, never offends anybody, has a smile for one and all. He has lived for himself at his own expense. Everybody greets him affectionately. But I, a harsh farmer, severe, stingy, and truculent, took a wife. Plenty of trouble there! Fathered two sons—more trouble. When I worked hard to provide for them, I wore out my life in striving. Now that I've reached old age, here's the reward they give me for my hard work—their dislike. This brother of mine reaps the rewards of fatherhood without any effort. They adore him but shun me. They confide all their plans to him; they love him. They both stay with him, while I'm deserted. They pray for his long life, but I suppose they're hoping for my death. Thus he makes them both his own sons cheaply, although they have been brought up by me at great expense. I get all the bother; he gets the pleasure. So come now, let us take the opposite track. Since he's issuing me a challenge, let's see if I can talk pleasantly and act kindly. I also want to be loved and be well thought of by my boys. If this requires generosity and tolerance, I'll not be behindhand. The money will run out, but at my advanced age that scarcely matters. (855ff.)

And so it appears that Demea has undergone a change of heart, a veritable transformation of the personality such as that experienced by Cnemon in *Dyscolus*. But the sequel shows that matters are not so simple. At first sight it seems that such will be the case, as Demea greets first Syrus, and then another slave named Geta, with unwonted affability, treating them virtually as equals. After he has done so, he says in a self-satisfied aside, "I am gradually winning the lower classes over to my side" (898).

Then he meets Aeschines, and with an uncharacteristic display of emotions announces that he is his son's father both by birth and by nature, and that he loves him more than his own eyes (902f.).

But matters quickly swerve in a different direction. Demea is increasingly generous. When Aeschines complains that the wedding is being delayed, Demea airily responds that there is no problem—just break down the wall separating Micio's house from Sostrata's and combine the families into one. In an aside to the audience Demea reveals his real thinking (911): of course he can be as generous as he wants, for he is purchasing his own new popularity with Micio's money.

Micio, finding out that the wall is being demolished, breaks out of the house in fury, but Demea in his newly benign way convinces him that he should indeed support Sostrata's family. Indeed, with Aeschines breathlessly seconding him, he proposes all sorts of ways in which Micio can be generous: an estate for Hegio, freedom for Syrus, his wife, and Geta. Come to think of it, Micio ought to settle down and marry Sostrata.

Micio is of course appalled, both by seeing his money evanesce and at the prospect of losing his bachelor freedom to marry a woman he frankly regards as "a decrepit hag" (938). Finally, when he has finished rubbing Micio's and Aeschines' noses in this outburst of extravagant generosity, he brings home the lesson in a speech at 985ff.:

> I'll tell you why I acted thus. In order to show to you that the reason these boys think you are liberal and affable, Micio, does not come from the way you live your life or for any good and reasonable reason, but because of your permissiveness, your indulgence, and your open purse. And now, Aeschines, if my life style is hateful to you because I do not give in to you completely on every matter, just and unjust alike, I'm done with the subject. Spend, squander, do what you like. But because of your youth you are heedless in your desires and excessively eager, and you may wish me to reprove and correct you on occasion as well as support you. If so, here I am at your service.

Aeschines can only say that henceforth he will defer to Demea. Demea says that he will allow Ctesipho to keep Bacchis—but that this must be his last fling. Micio chimes in this is right, and the play thus ends.

The issue explored in *Adelphoe*, the proposition that upbringing shapes character and that differing forms of upbringing create different products, is distinctly reminiscent of the theme of *The Clouds*, although one of the play's special jokes is that *Adelphoe* suggests that the products of different upbringings needn't be so very different after all. Since we are shown two allegedly contrasting products of conservative and liberal, old-fashioned and modern upbringings, *Adelphoe* even more sharply recalls *The Banqueteers*. Perhaps this is no accident. In a more general sense, the play very certainly is a commentary on a host of comedies of the *Mostellaria* type that favorably contrast liberality and hedonism, located in the city, with repressive conservatism, situated in the countryside.

To the extent that *Adelphoe* is conceived as a commentary on these two Aristophanic plays and perhaps other comedies treating the same theme, its message is that things are not so simple as comedy traditionally represents them.

This is true regarding both the play's central issue and its characters. Given the history of ancient comedy, one would predict both that it would show that different methods of child rearing would produce different kinds of young men, and that the more tolerant method would be represented as unquestionably superior. In that sense, the spectator expecting to see yet another rehearsal of comedy's standard lesson about the superiority of the young at heart and the fun-loving has lit up an exploding cigar. The play explores the limitations and deficiencies of tolerant liberality and strongly suggests that a hedonistic approach to life is not without its own shortcomings. The play's critical attitude toward liberalism and hedonism is startlingly new and different.

In *Adelphoe* we are shown a familiar cast of characters. Many of its major characters have generic equivalents in *Mostellaria*. In accordance with comedy's usual antiauthoritarian and fun-loving outlook, the position represented by Micio would normally be characterized as entirely in the right, and that represented by Demea would be given some manner of unsympathetic representation. Demea himself, in the tradition of such characters as Theopropides in *Mostellaria*, would be portrayed as an agelast and would be assigned some such unpleasant traits as dourness, excessive austerity, or obtuseness, and Micio, a fun-loving older man of the Simo type, would be presented as a decidedly more attractive human being. The play would conclude with the decisive and uncomplicated triumph of the fun-loving characters and the values they represent.

But in accordance with Terence's program of heightened realism, representing life in something resembling its full complexity, things do not work out this way. There is plenty to be said in favor of Demea's conservative approach and his philosophy of child rearing. In agreement with this revised way of regarding the situation, Demea is given a sympathetic characterization. There is nothing pathological about him, and for a "repressive" comic father he is, very uncharacteristically, not shown as either stupid or insensitive. Indeed, by the end of the play we appreciate that he is its most intelligent character. He conceives and executes a plan for turning the tables on Micio and teaching him and the two boys a valuable lesson about hedonism's limitations. Although Micio already seems to have some doubts about the wisdom of keeping such a loose rein on adolescent men, he keeps his reservations to himself. Demea pushes the issue to extremes to make Micio confront the issue squarely. But it is the mark of Demea's tact and intelligence that he manages to do so in such a way that Micio is not subject to undue humiliation and so that no attempt is made to alienate the boys' affections or interfere with their love lives. *Adelphoe* is not a comedy that ends with a typical reconciliation of its characters, because no such reconciliation is needed. Demea has engineered a solution in which everybody (even plenty of secondary characters) wins.

Adelphoe is populated with a set of characters quite unlike any we have previously encountered. They are equipped with a remarkable repertoire of emotions. They blush; they cry; they are capable of feeling and of expressing deep affection. The need to be loved is recognized as a necessary human desire. There is no room here for Oedipus. This is the only comedy we have read in which the relation of a son (or at least an adopted son) and his father is portrayed as loving rather than antagonistic, so that we are shown the possibility that a *familia* can be held together by bonds of affection rather than by upward-directed loyalty and downward-directed authoritarianism. His characters are moved by genuine feelings (although Terence is no mawkish sentimentalist). They are capable of learning and growing, and an important part of Terence's interest in psychological analysis is the representation of human character evolving in response to changing circumstance. In *Dyscolus* this can be said of the central character, but in *Adelphoe* the observation holds good not just for Demea but also for those who are educated by his trick.

There is, in short, an unusual degree of sophistication in *Adelphoe*. Neither its issues nor its characters are represented in a simplistic or one-sided way. Terence has converted comedy into an instrument for a more serious and realistic exploration of life's problems and of human nature. Comedy perennially pokes fun at sacred cows, but it turns out that ancient comedy has a certain sacred cow of its own. In *Adelphoe* Terence calls into question a view that constitutes the central feature of ancient comedy's characteristic world-view: uncritical and reflexive endorsement of hedonism. "Yes, but life does not really work like that" is not a message characteristic of comedy, and when this comment is made about hedonism the result is rather devastating. If comedy is a subversive literary form, Terence turns the tables and writes a kind of drama meant to subvert comedy itself. And so there is a fine symbolism in the fact that *Adelphoe* (together with the *Hecyra*, produced in the same year, just prior to Terence's death) happens to be the last ancient comedy to be written surviving from antiquity.

In his recent book on Terence,[3] Sander M. Goldberg observes that the death of Terence meant, for all intents and purposes, the death of comedy at Rome. This presents the literary historian with a puzzle. Why did Roman comedy cease to flourish at a time when Roman literature as a whole was, if not still quite in its infancy, at least in its early and rather ungainly adolescence? Probably any number of causes might be discovered for comedy's early demise, but surely part of the responsibility (or should one say the blame?) falls on Terence himself. Goldberg plausibly suggests that Terence's innovations had the effect of alienating comedy from itself. Thus an argument might be constructed parallel to that of Aristophanes in *The Frogs* (revived by Nietzsche in *The Birth of Tragedy*) that Euripides' innovations had the effect of killing Greek tragedy. Some of the innovations in question were rather similar to those introduced by Terence: use of drama as a subtle tool for the critical examination of issues and exploration of character, coupled with a new toleration of moral ambiguities. Probably the motivation was also somewhat similar for both playwrights. Although they were still ostensibly writing for production in the popular theater, they were (much more than their respective predecessors) writing plays to be seen and read by a rising class of educated intellectuals; in Terence's case this was the Scipionic circle.

Goldberg's essential complaint is that Terence's ironical probing of character and social relationships took the fun out of comedy. He could have added that, since the quest for fun and freedom is the great ground-theme of ancient comedy, adoption of a detached and critical attitude toward hedonism, coupled with the insight that those who would put the brakes on fun-seeking are not necessarily in the wrong, is not only uncomic but downright anticomic. The construction of a critique of hedonism may well be a sign of deeper wisdom and increased moral and intellectual sophistication. But it is fatal to the spirit of comedy. Thus the difficulty with Terence is not just that his plays are insufficiently hilarious or lacking in comic energy, as modern critics often complain. The real problem is that at their very heart is a philosophy of life that is incompatible with the innate outlook of ancient comedy. After Terence, there really was nowhere for comedy to go.

Notes and References

CHAPTER 1

1. Article "Dionysia" in C. Daremberg and E. Saglio, *Dictionnaire des Antiquités Greques et Romaines* (Paris, 1892) 2.232f. (my translation).

2. Aristophanes wrote a total of twenty-four plays. In later antiquity interest in Old Comedy was distinctly limited (his greatest fan was the satirical Lucian). His plays were studied in rhetorical schools for the purity of their classical Attic Greek more than for their contents, and this helps to explain why only some plays by him, and none by anybody else, survive.

3. *Shakespeare's Festive Comedy: A Study of Dramatic Form and its Relation to Social Custom* (Princeton, 1959).

4. Ibid. 37.

5. Examples: the *Seventh Homeric Hymn*; Aeschylus' lost play *The Edonians* (preserved in fragments only, including those of its Roman adaptation, Naevius' *Lycurgus*); the version of the Lycurgus myth told at Diodorus Siculus 3.66; the hymn to Dionysus (III c. A.D.) preserved by the papyrus *P. Ross. Georg.* 1.11. Cf. my discussions of these items at "Aeschylus' *Edonians*," in *Fons Perennis: Saggi Critici di Filologia Classica Raccoliti in Onore del Professore Vittorio D'Agostino* (Turin, 1971) 387–411, and *Papyrological Studies in Dionysiac Literature* (Chicago, 1988) 87–96. (I would not dare place such interpretational significance on *The Bacchae* and *Cyclops*, of course, if I were not convinced that they were representative of a larger number of plays of their respective classes.)

6. Or, more precisely, tragedy was originally a moralistic genre, until Euripides began to employ it as a tool for exploring moral and ethical ambiguities in the later part of the fifth century B.C. In many ways, as Aristophanes vociferously complained in his *Frogs*, Euripides employed tragedy for new and unorthodox purposes.

7. Sir Kenneth Dover, *Aristophanic Comedy* (London, 1972), 125f.

8. Jeffrey C. Henderson, *The Maculate Muse* (New Haven, 1971), 172 states that *typto* can be used in this way, but the point has been challenged in a review by R. J. Bickerman, *Athenaeum* n.s. 56 (1978) 411 n.4. The argument that Pheidippides is threatening to "bang" or rape his mother has been made by Kenneth J. Reckford, "Father-Beating in Aristophanes' *Clouds*," in *The Conflict of Generations in Ancient Greece and Rome* (ed. S. Bertman, Amsterdam, 1976), 89–118, who however did not apply it to a reading of the play. Likewise Leo Strauss, *Socrates and Aristophanes* (London – New York, 1966) repeatedly referred to the incest innuendo in *Clouds* in the course of his first chapter, but did not develop the point.

CHAPTER 2

1. A word of caution must be issued here: no general study of the phenomenon of romantic love in antiquity has ever been written. So sweeping remarks such as this have to be regarded as somewhat provisional.

2. Old Comedy had also used masks, possibly even some standard ones, although doubtless many had to be specially constructed to look like actual people who were represented on the stage (Euripides, Socrates, etc.). But this new set of New Comedy stock masks appears to have had little if anything to do with the masks of Aristophanes' day.

3. Some of the most important discussions of this question are listed in the section on theoretical discussions in the Bibliographical Essay appended to this study.

4. It deserves to be pointed out that Aristotle wrote the *Poetics* in the fourth century B.C. and in that work, I believe, reflected the literary tastes and interests of his own time. Therefore, when he wrote about tragedy he did not necessarily give expression to the aims and aspirations of the great writers of Attic tragedy, who lived in the previous century.

5. On the other hand, a more appropriate modern television analogy for Aristophanes' comedies would be something like *Saturday Night Live* or *Monty Python's Flying Circus*, the first because of the promi-

nence of political satire, the second for the same reason, and also because of the frequent excursions into fantasy.

6. E. W. Handley, *The Dyskolos of Menander* (Cambridge, Mass., 1965), p. 190.

7. Douglas Domingo-Forasté, *"Piety in Menander,"* Laetaberis n. s. 7 (1989), 1–8. In his first footnote the author summarizes previous discussions of these letters.

8. Loeb, *Hesiod, The Homeric Hymns and Homerica* (trans. H. G. Evelyn-White, second ed., Cambridge, Mass. – London, 1936).

CHAPTER 3

1. Quoted from the Everyman Library edition, *A History of Rome* (trans. W. P. Dixon, London – Toronto – New York, 1911), 2.399–418.

2. Ibid. 403.

3. Ibid. 415.

4. For these texts, cf. above all E. W. Handley, *Menander and Plautus: A Study in Comparison* (London, 1968).

5. Both texts are quoted as translated by Norma Miller, *Menander's Plays and Fragments* (Penguin ed., London, 1987), 178f.

6. Erich Segal, *Roman Laughter* (Cambridge, Mass., 1978).

7. Alice Lotvin Birney, *Satiric Catharsis in Shakespeare: A Theory in Dramatic Structure* (Berkeley, 1973) is an example.

8. Cf. Mommsen, *History of Rome*, 2.371–89 (chap. 8) and G. Colin, *Rome et la Grèce de 200 à 146 av. J.-C.* (Paris, 1905).

9. H. H. Scullard, *Roman Politics 220–150 B.C.* (New York, 1951): cf. esp. 133ff.

10. *Tropaeum Liberi* (Genoa, 1957).

11. This reading of course requires the assumption that the same techniques of displacement, disguise, and indirect representation that Sigmund Freud detected as mechanisms of the "dream work" can also function in drama and narrative literature.

12. Holt Parker, "Crucially Funny or Tranio on the Couch: The *Servus Callidus* and Jokes about Torture," *Transactions of the American Philological Association* 119 (1989), 233–246; the quotation is from 245f.

13. My own ideas about comic catharsis will be set forth in *The Catharsis of Comedy*, forthcoming from Rowman and Littlefield.

CHAPTER 4

1. Of course, in his handling of character depiction he may have been following the lead of the Greek originals he was adapting. But in the absence of information about his originals, we must speak as if this were his innovation.

2. According to Athenian law, a woman had to have a legal guardian at all times. Normally she passed from the tutelage of her father to that of her husband, but if the father died such a marriage to a kinswoman would be enforced. This legal arrangement, enjoining unwanted marriages, is a plot element in several New and Roman Comedies (e.g., Terence's *Phormio*).

3. Sander M. Goldberg, in the final chapter of the work listed in the bibliographical essay.

Bibliographical Essay

My aim here is to list studies mainly of interest to the nonspecialist. Accordingly, only works in the English language are mentioned, and I focus on general studies rather than on articles in specialized scholarly journals. The reason that many more book-length studies are listed for the Greek side than the Roman reflects the fact that contemporary classical scholarship is dominated by Hellenists. I can take this limited approach with confidence because reasonably up-to-date bibliographies, which include references to specialized bibliographical publications, are appended to the respective volumes of the *Cambridge History of Classical Literature*, as noted below.

THEORETICAL DISCUSSIONS

There is no single theoretical discussion of comedy that can be recommended wholeheartedly, but the reader can extract many useful concepts from such works as Willard Smith, *The Nature of Comedy* (Boston, 1930), Maurice Cheney, *Comedy High and Low* (Oxford, 1968), and Elder Olson, *The Theory of Comedy* (Bloomington, Ind., 1968). The concept of festive comedy set forth by C. L. Barber's *Shakespeare's Festive Comedy: A Study of Dramatic Form and its Relation to Social Custom* (Princeton, 1959) has been applied to both Greek and Roman comedy. Readers who care to pursue this approach will also find useful M. M. Bakhtin, *Rabelais and his World* (trans. H. Iswolsky, Cambridge, Mass., 1968).

Comedy is only a subdivision of humor, and there also exists a large literature on humor in general, asking what makes people laugh and why. Some interesting discussions include Joyce O. Hertzler, *Laughter: A Socio-Scientific Analysis* (New York, 1970), Norman. N. Holland, *Laughing: A Psychology of Humor* (Ithaca, 1982), Helmuth Plessner, *Laughing and Crying* (third ed., trans. J. S. Churchill and M. Grene, Evanston, 1970). Some of C. L. Barber's theoretical understanding of the workings of festive comedy depends on Sigmund Freud's *Der Witz und siene Bezeihung zum Unbewußten* (Leipzig-Vienna, 1905, second ed. 1912), translated under the title *Jokes and their Relation to the Unconscious* by James Strachey as volume 8 of the Standard Edition of Freud's works (London, 1960). Martin Grotjahn, *Beyond Laughter: Humor and the Subconscious* (New York, 1957) is a modern Freudian study.

If Aristotle did indeed discuss comedy in a lost second half of the *Poetics*, one naturally wants to know what he said. The two most important studies of this topic are Lane Cooper, *An Aristotelian Theory of Comedy* (New York, 1922) and Richard Janko, *Aristotle on Comedy* (Berkeley, 1985). Both of these works are perforce speculative, and it might not be unfair to say that Cooper, who was not a classicist, was more interested in developing a set of concepts for contemporary use than in making an archaeological reconstruction of Aristotle's thinking. But these observations are not meant to detract from the interest or value of either work. I shall discuss comic catharsis at length in *The Catharsis of Comedy*, forthcoming in the series "Greek Studies: Interdisciplinary Approaches" (edited by Gregory Nagy), to be published by Rowman and Littlefield.

DRAMATIC PRODUCTION

The reader presumably wants to know about Greek comedy's festival context, the comic competitions, the available resources of the Greek theater, and how the plays were actually staged. As a teacher, I am not in the habit of recommending "study guide" type surveys. But I gladly make an exception for Meyer Reinhold's *Classical Drama, Greek and Roman* (in Barron's Educational

Series, Woodbury, N.Y., 1959). Reinhold manages to include an amazing amount of information, with sections pertinent to dramatic production and every other subject touched on here (the appended bibliography is of course very much in need of updating). Other and more detailed studies include Margarete Bieber, *The History of the Greek and Roman Theater* (second ed., Princeton, 1961), Roy C. Flickinger, *The Greek Theater and its Drama* (fourth ed., Chicago, 1936), Sir Arthur Pickard-Cambridge, *The Theater of Dionysus in Athens* (Oxford, 1946), and T. B. L. Webster, *Greek Theater Production* (second ed., London, 1970).

GENERAL STUDIES OF GREEK COMEDY

Before turning to Aristophanes, one may mention a few studies pertaining to Greek comedy in general. F. M. Sandbach's *The Comic Theater of Greece and Rome* (New York, 1977) is very unusual in that it treats both Greek and Roman comedy in a single volume; however, the author makes no effort to investigate resemblances between earlier and later comedy. A first-rate overview of all Greek comedy, from its origins through Menander and the New Comedy, is provided in the chapter on comedy by E. W. Handley in volume 1 of the *Cambridge History of Classical Literature* (eds. P. E. Easterling and B. M. W. Knox, Cambridge, U.K., 1985), 355–425; cf. also the bibliography at 773–783. The section devoted to comedy in Sir Arthur Pickard-Cambridge's *Dithyramb, Tragedy, and Comedy* (Oxford, 1927) provides much excellent material about Old Comedy's origins and nature. If possible, this book should be read in its original edition rather than in the second edition (Oxford, 1962), revised posthumously by T. B. L. Webster. In this latter edition Webster sometimes silently substituted his own opinions for those of Pickard-Cambridge. The same author's *The Dramatic Festivals at Athens* (second ed., Oxford, 1968), 57ff., provides a useful description of the Dionysiac festivals. G. Sifakis' *Parabasis and Animal Chorus* (London, 1971) is an interesting study of Old Comedy choruses. Gilbert Norwood's *Greek Comedy* (London, 1931) is chiefly valuable for all the material it contains about lost works by Aristophanes and other comic poets (the section on Menander is of course very obsolete because of the discovery of many new papyri). On the other hand, the reader should be specifically warned away from J. M. Edmonds, *The*

Fragments of Attic Comedy (Leiden, 1957–1961). This three-volume edition of the fragments of lost plays, with facing English translation, was done by an eccentric who let his imagination run fast and free, with the result that his presentation of the evidence is often very unreliable.

ARISTOPHANES: GENERAL STUDIES

B. B. Rogers's translation, available in the Loeb Classical Library series with explanatory notes added by John Williams White (three vols., London – Cambridge, Mass., 1924), is done in the style of W. S. Gilbert, not inappropriately since Gilbert was a close student of Aristophanes' meters. This version is prim and proper. The prosaic anonymous translations (rumored to be the work of Gilbert Murray) printed in the second volume of the Random House *The Complete Greek Drama* set (eds. Whitney F. Oates and Eugene O'Neill, Jr., New York, 1938) are not. For a modern set of Greek texts with facing translations, introductions, and commentaries one can use the set by D. Barrett (*The Wasps, The Birds, The Thesmophoriazusae, The Frogs, The Ecclesiazusae*) and Alan Sommerstein (*The Acharnians, The Clouds, Peace, Lysistrata, Plutus*) (Warminster, 1964–79).

As one might imagine, the number of book-length general studies of Aristophanic comedy is very large. Here I shall only mention the most useful modern ones. K. J. Dover's *Aristophanic Comedy* (London, 1972) is a very good starting point. Cedric H. Whitman's *Aristophanes and the Comic Hero* (Cambridge, Mass., 1964) provides an interesting look at Aristophanes' central characters. But the study is flawed and raises as many questions as it answers: Whitman calls these characters heroic without giving any adequate account of their heroism, and he pays insufficient attention to the factors that differentiate them from their opponents. In the past decade several general studies have appeared that reflect advances in contemporary comic criticism and so tend to be a good deal more penetrating than their predecessors. Rosemary M. Harrott's *Aristophanes, Poet and Dramatist* (London, 1982), looks at dramatic, poetic, and narrative techniques. Kenneth J. Reckford's *Aristophanes' Old and New Comedy I: Six Essays in Perspective* (Chapel Hill, N.C., 1987), is the first volume of what promises to be an enormous study. The author throws out innumerable ideas, and I am very indebted to Reckford's way of looking at comedy, especially to his willingness to use psychological insights. Kenneth McLeish's *The Theatre of Aristophanes* (London, 1980) also looks at the poet's dramatic technique. Dana F. Sutton's *Self and Society in Aristophanes* (Washington, D.C., 1980) applies C. L. Barber's theory of festive comedy to Aristophanes. Jeffrey Henderson's *The Maculate Muse* (New Haven, 1975) looks at the poet's use of obscenity. The first section of the study is a theoretical discussion written from a psychoanalytic viewpoint. The second and larger part is a detailed examination of such language. Even a Greekless reader can learn much from it. C. W. Deardon's *The Stage of Aristophanes* (London, 1975), looks at Aristophanes' stage technique. For the poet's political orientation, the reader might care to look at G. E. M. de Ste Croix, *The Origins of the Peloponnesian War* (London, 1972), appendix 29, "The Political Outlook of Aristophanes," and Malcom Heath, *Political Comedy in Aristophanes* (Göttingen, 1987).

INDIVIDUAL PLAYS

The best thing ever published about *The Wasps* is the introduction, Greek text, and commentary by D. M. MacDowell (Oxford, 1971). Even those with no knowledge of Greek can learn a great deal from this work. The reader may also be interested in Kenneth J. Reckford, "Catharsis and Dream—Interpretation in Aristophanes' *Wasps*," *Transactions of the American Philological Association* 107 (1977) 283ff.

The Clouds, as one might imagine, has generated a great deal more literature because of its "Socrates problem." Again, even the Greekless reader can profit from the introductions and commentaries by K. J. Dover (Oxford, 1968) and Alan Sommerstein (Warminster, 1982), the latter with facing English translation. Individual studies include Kenneth J. Reckford, "Father-Beating in Aristophanes' *Clouds,*" in *The Conflict of Generations in Ancient Greece and Rome* (ed. S. Bertman, Amsterdam, 1976), 89–118; the reader interested in generational conflict will find the other essays in this collection helpful. Raymond K. Fisher's *Aristo-*

phanes' Clouds: *Purpose and Technique* (Amsterdam, 1989) is a highly informative study of the whole play. The reader interested in the Socrates question might care to read Leo Strauss, *Socrates and Aristophanes* (London – New York, 1966).

NEW COMEDY AND MENANDER

The best introduction to later Greek comedy is T. B. L. Webster, *Studies in Later Greek Comedy* (second ed., Manchester, 1969).

For a translation of Menander, Norma Miller's *Menander, Plays and Fragments* (London 1987, in the Penguin series) can be highly recommended. W. G. Arnott's new version of Menander for the Loeb Classical Library (Cambridge, Mass., and London, 1979–) is also excellent. As I write, only the first volume of a projected three-volume series is available. Again, the Greekless reader will profit greatly from E. W. Handley's commentary on *Dyscolus* (London, 1965) and also from A. W. Gomme and F. H. Sandbach, *Menander: A Commentary* (Oxford, 1973), a critical commentary on all the surviving Menander material. Volume-length critical studies of Menander include T. B. L. Webster, *Studies in Menander* (second ed., London, 1960), the same author's *An Introduction to Menander* (Manchester, 1974), and Sander M. Goldberg, *The Making of Menander's Comedy* (London, 1980). For Menander and his Roman progeny, cf. W. G. Arnott, *Menander, Plautus, and Terence* (Oxford, 1975). R. L. Hunter's *The New Comedy of Greece and Rome* (Cambridge, U.K., 1987) is an instructive study of later classical drama in general. E. W. Handley's *Menander and Plautus: A Study in Comparison* (London, 1968) has been described as the single most important contribution to Plautine studies in this century, since for the first time we can study how a Roman comic poet adapted his Greek source.

ROMAN COMEDY

There is a section on Roman drama in Bieber's work listed in the section on dramatic production above, but the most comprehensive survey of Roman theatrical life ever written is W. Beare's enormously informative *The Roman Stage* (third ed., London, 1964). A useful introduction is George E. Duckworth, *The Nature of Roman Comedy: A Study in Popular Entertainment* (Princeton, 1951). R. L. Hunter's work has been noted in the previous section. We now also have the survey by A. S. Gratwick in the second volume of the *Cambridge History of Classical Literature* (Cambridge, U.K., 1982), 95ff., with an appended bibliography on 808ff. (For a post-1982 update, cf. Slater's bibliography for Plautus and those by Forehand and Goldberg for Terence in the works listed below).

PLAUTUS

While there are any number of available translations of individual plays or selections (two good volumes in the Penguin series, for example), for the complete works one should use the highly readable versions of Paul Nixon in the Loeb Classical Library series (five volumes, Cambridge, Mass., and London, 1916–1938).

As indicated in the text, Erich Segal's *Roman Laughter: The Comedy of Plautus* (Cambridge, Mass., 1978) is a highly important study. The fact that, as stated in the text, I disagree with the author's understanding of Barber's theory of festival comedy scarcely diminishes my respect for this work or its importance in the history of criticism of Plautus. Since Segal, other particularly penetrating general studies have been written, notably Netta Zagagi, *Tradition and Originality in Plautus* (Göttingen, 1980), David Constan, *Roman Comedy* (Ithaca, 1983), which is primarily about Plautus but contains two essays devoted to Terence, and most recently Niall W. Slater, *Plautus in Performance: The Theatre of the Mind* (Princeton, 1985), who is particularly alive to the way Plautine comedy would play on the stage.

I must acknowledge my particular debt to Holt Parker, "Crucially Funny or Tranio on the Couch: The *Servus Callidus* and Jokes about Torture," *Transactions of the American Philological Association* 119 (1989), 233–246, not so much because of the author's specific conclusions as because the kind of psychological reading he applies to Plautus strikes me as enormously fruitful. On the other hand, the kind of sociopolitical reading I have suggested is not very much reflected in the literature, because few modern students of Plautus seem interested in reading his plays against the specific historical situation in which they were written.

TERENCE

A good set of translations is Betty Radice, *Terence: The Comedies* (London, 1965).

Among book-length studies, Gilbert Norwood's *The Art of Terence* (Oxford, 1923) retains its interest. More modern general studies include John Wright, *Dancing in Chains: The Stylistic Unity of the "Comoedia Palliata"* (Papers and Monographs of the American Academy at Rome 25, Rome, 1974), Walter E. Forehand, *Terence* (Twayne's World Authors Series, Boston, 1985), and Sander M. Goldberg, *Understanding Terence* (Princeton, 1986).

AUDIO AND VIDEO PERFORMANCES

Audio and video performances of and commentaries on many of the authors and plays discussed in this volume are available from such companies as:

Audio-Forum
96 Broad Street
Guilford, CT 06437

Films for the Humanities
743 Alexander Road
Princeton, NJ 08540

Videologue
Trade Service Company
10996 Torreyana Road
San Diego, CA 92121

Most video stores specializing in arts and humanities will provide information on titles currently available.

Index

About the Author

Dana F. Sutton was born in 1942 and received the Ph.D. from the University of Wisconsin in 1970. The recipient of a 1975 Guggenheim Fellowship, Professor Sutton has written and lectured widely about Greek and Roman poetry and drama. Currently Professor of Classics and Chair of the Department of Classics at the University of California, Irvine, he is the author of such works as *The Greek Satyr Play* (1980), *Self and Society in Aristophanes* (1980), *The Lost Sophocles* (1984), and *Seneca on the Stage* (1986).